HV

W9-DEV-834

2005

ARE EFFORTS TO REDUCE TERRORISM SUCCESSFUL?

Lauri S. Friedman, *Book Editor*

Bruce Glassman, *Vice President*
Bonnie Szumski, *Publisher*
Helen Cothran, *Managing Editor*

GREENHAVEN PRESS
An imprint of Thomson Gale, a part of The Thomson Corporation

Detroit • New York • San Francisco • San Diego • New Haven, Conn.
Waterville, Maine • London • Munich

LIBRARY OF CONGRESS CATALOGING-IN-PUBLICATION DATA

Are efforts to reduce terrorism successful? / Lauri S. Friedman, book editor.
    p. cm. — (At issue)
    Includes bibliographical references and index.
    ISBN 0-7377-2334-3 (lib. : alk. paper) — ISBN 0-7377-2335-1 (pbk. : alk. paper)
    1. Terrorism—United States—Prevention. 2. Terrorism—Government policy—United States. 3. War on Terrorism, 2001– . I. Friedman, Lauri S. II. Series: At issue (San Diego, Calif.)
    HV6432.A74 2005
    363.32'0973—dc22
                                                             2004042421

Printed in the United States of America

Contents

Introduction

Scoring the war on terror is a complicated task for most Americans. On any given day, they can skim a variety of news sources and get very different impressions about its status. By some accounts, the war is being won on its many fronts; by other accounts, it is a most miserable failure. An additional reason Americans find it difficult to judge the war is that much of it is being conducted secretly for security reasons. As this volume goes to press, no further terrorist attacks have occurred on American soil since September 11, 2001—another fact that makes it difficult to assess the war on terror. It either means that the war has been successful or simply that no new attacks have been attempted. Although the war on terrorism may be hard to evaluate, it is undeniable that Americans are vested in it. Either with criticism or compliments, everyone is talking about the efforts to reduce terrorism.

The attacks of September 11, 2001, shook the nation to its core and challenged the prevailing notion that America was invulnerable to attack. Only a handful of people could have predicted that terrorists would have used airplanes as flying bombs to unleash terror and devastation on American soil. In the immediate aftermath of the attacks, which killed over three thousand people, money was poured into the airline industry to prevent other jets from being hijacked in the same way.

It soon became clear, however, that much more than just the airline industry needed protection from terrorism. Indeed, it did not take officials long to develop a list of sectors of society that were, on closer inspection, dangerously vulnerable to attack. The nearly eight thousand miles of borders the United States shares with Mexico and Canada were uncomfortably open, as were its twelve thousand miles of coastline. The nation's trucking, rail lines, and nuclear power plants also had very little security in place. National landmarks also seemed particularly defenseless; American treasures, such as Mount Rushmore and Ellis Island, appeared especially prone to attack because of their symbolic value. To take on the enormous task of safeguarding the nation, the Department of Homeland Security was created in the months following September 11.

Among the daunting tasks the new department is responsible for is figuring out exactly who is in the country, and with what intentions. America is an open society, one that values individual privacy and freedom of choice and movement. Indeed, because of these qualities, America has traditionally been a beacon of freedom and opportunity to those around the world. After September 11, however, living in an open society seemed suddenly like a liability rather than an asset. After all, the September 11 terrorists had used legal channels to enter the country. Officials realized that radically new approaches would be needed to apprehend terrorists who had managed to blend into society.

Part of the sweeping changes that occurred after September 11 thus affected privacy and freedom. The USA PATRIOT Act was adopted, which expands government powers and intelligence capabilities in order to ferret out terrorists living in the United States. Another program, called Total Information Awareness (TIA), was also developed to enhance intelligence capabilities and gather information about the civilian population. These two programs have met mixed reactions; some people appreciate efforts to scrutinize the population and claim they have nothing to hide; others complain that the new measures violate the civil liberties of ordinary Americans and contend that such breaches of privacy have little to do with counterterrorism.

In addition to changes at home, the war on terror immediately spread overseas. Indeed, stamping out foreign-born terrorism became a key tenet of U.S. policy. To this end, in October 2001 U.S. and coalition forces ousted the fundamentalist Taliban government of Afghanistan. Many Americans saw this war as a direct retaliation for the September 11 attacks, as the Taliban had sheltered September 11 mastermind Osama bin Laden. In 2003 U.S. forces fought another war in Iraq to overthrow dictator Saddam Hussein. The Bush administration claimed that his regime was building weapons of mass destruction and had ties to terrorist groups. These military incursions made clear that America would be active abroad in its war on terrorism. A variety of operations continue overseas in a multitude of countries that are linked to terrorism in some way. Pakistan, the Philippines, Saudi Arabia, Libya, North Korea, Indonesia, and Europe are just some of the places where the United States has undertaken military, intelligence, and diplomatic operations relating to its war on terror.

Although monumental changes have taken place since September 11, it remains, on the whole, unclear whether these efforts to reduce terrorism are indeed working. In fact, a dizzying array of conclusions has been drawn, making it nearly impossible to achieve consensus on the effectiveness of the war. For example, President George W. Bush, one of the most vocal supporters of the war on terrorism, claims that terrorists are being caught and thus the war on terrorism is succeeding. As he said in his State of the Union address in January 2003, "We have the terrorists on the run. We're keeping them on the run. One by one, the terrorists are learning the meaning of American justice." *National Review* contributor Kate O'Beirne agrees, confidently lauding the achievements of the war on terrorism:

> In the past two years, terrorist cells in Buffalo, Detroit, Seattle, and Portland, Ore., have been dismantled; criminal charges have been brought against 225 suspected terrorists; and 132 of those suspects have been convicted. Terrorists haven't carried out another attack here because the domestic war on terrorism, aimed at prevention, has worked.

Other observers, however, look at the same list of accomplishments and conclude that when one terrorist is removed, a hundred step up to take his or her place. Author Scott Holleran, contributor to *Capitalism Magazine*, argued this point in a September 8, 2003, article entitled "Why We're Losing the War on Terror":

> The White House has made much of the fact that two-thirds of al Qaeda's leadership has been caught. Picking off top ter-

rorists one by one will not win this war. As one Taliban fighter scoffed, when asked by the Associated Press to comment on [al] Qaeda leader Khalid Sheikh Mohammed's capture: "There are lots of people who can do his work."

Indeed, critics of the war on terrorism believe it has in fact enlarged the terrorist problem and inspired more terrorists to take up arms against the United States. In her August 20, 2003, article "How America Created a Terrorist Haven," *New York Times* reporter Jessica Stern wrote:

> [The] bombing of the United Nations headquarters in Baghdad [Iraq] was the latest evidence that America has taken a country that was not a terrorist threat and turned it into one. . . . The occupation [of Iraq by American troops] has given disparate groups from various countries a common battlefield on which to fight a common enemy.

Thus, measuring success seems to be a matter of how one interprets the facts. Because of this, evaluating the war on terrorism is very complicated.

Another factor preventing the public from determining whether efforts to reduce terrorism have been successful has to do with secrecy. Many of the details of the war on terrorism are kept secret, in large part for security reasons. For example, if intelligence officers are able to infiltrate terrorist cells and make key arrests, those arrests will need to be kept from the public so as to prevent the enemy from learning who among them has been captured. Indeed, only a very select group of high ranking officials will even be aware that certain operations are ongoing. President Bush acknowledged this necessity when he addressed Congress on September 20, 2001, saying, "Our response [to the attacks of September 11, 2001] involves far more than instant retaliation and isolated strikes. Americans should not expect one battle, but a lengthy campaign, unlike any other we have ever seen. It may include dramatic strikes, visible on TV, and covert operations, secret even in success."

These secret fronts of the war on terror make it difficult to gauge its success, and it remains nearly impossible for the average citizen to monitor the war's progress. This secrecy has elicited many different reactions from Americans; some have supported the claim that secrecy is necessary. These Americans trust that their government will protect them as best it can. The secrecy has not boded well with others, however, who are accustomed to living in an open society where their government's actions are subject to public scrutiny.

Perhaps the most difficult challenge facing those trying to evaluate the war is its ambiguous nature: Does the absence of attacks in the United States indicate that security measures are working, or that attacks have not been attempted? The absence of terrorism at home is indeed an eerie and confusing phenomenon. In late 2002 author Bill Powell pondered this predicament in an article for *Fortune* magazine:

> It has been a year since September 11 . . . and nothing has happened since. For all the warnings, for all the rumors of imminent dirty nukes, arrests of shoe bombers, and suspected sleeper cells, there has not, remarkably, been another attack. Not many people a year ago would have pre-

dicted that. It would be nice, therefore, to think that nothing like what happened then could happen now. That the merciful quiet at home in the year since the 11th has been because we have taken the war to the enemy abroad and become vigilant and smart at home.

In many ways, Americans can only speculate on whether efforts to reduce terrorism have met with success. While the efforts to prevent terrorism are visible all around us, their efficacy may not be definitively known until there is another attack. It is only then that changes to security will receive their first true test, and whatever weaknesses were left unaddressed will be made horribly clear. The viewpoints presented in *At Issue: Are Efforts to Reduce Terrorism Successful?* explore the gamut of actions being taken in the war against terrorism and offer insight into the wide range of interpretations of their success.

1

America Is Winning the War on Terrorism

George W. Bush

George W. Bush is the forty-third president of the United States.

America is making great strides in its war against those who hate freedom. Terrorists have been captured all over the world. The United States successfully liberated Afghanistan, which is no longer a haven for terror. Similarly, American soldiers freed Iraq, and in doing so made the world more secure. The United States opposes terrorists and all who support them, and it will not rest until the terrorist network is destroyed.

Editor's Note: The following remarks were addressed to military personnel and their families at a base in Southern California to commemorate their return home from service in the 2003 war in Iraq.

I'm honored to be in the presence of the men and women who wear our nation's uniform. I'm proud of you, and I want to thank you for your service to our great country. Each of you serves in a crucial time in our nation's history. And this nation is grateful for the sacrifice and service you make.

Many of you have recently returned from Iraq [after the 2003 war], and it seems like you're happy to be home. More than 70,000 men and women from bases in Southern California were deployed in Iraq. You served with honor. You served with skill. And you were successful.

Before you went in, Iraqis were an oppressed people, and the dictator [Saddam Hussein] threatened his neighbors, the Middle East and the world. Today, the Iraqis are liberated people, the former regime is gone, and our nation and the world is more secure.

This nation is at war with people who hate what we stand for. We love freedom, and we're not going to change. Our country depends on you to protect our freedom, and every day, you depend on your families. This has been a challenging time for military families. I know that. Dur-

George W. Bush, address to military personnel and families, San Diego, California, August 14, 2003.

ing the last year, our families and our military have met hardships, and met them together. You've supported and looked out for one another. You've been strong and faithful to the people you love. Military families make tremendous sacrifices for America, and our nation is grateful for your service to our country. . . .

An unrelenting campaign

The Marine Corps Air Station and the military bases of Southern California have long, long been crucial to the defense of this country. We intend to keep it that way. Generations of Marines, and sailors, and pilots have trained and served here. And for the veterans who are with us today, I thank you for your service to our country.

Now, you have been called. This group of Marines and sailors have been called to serve in the first war of the 21st century. The war began almost two years ago, on September the 11th, 2001, when this nation was brutally attacked and thousands of our fellow citizens died. We were awakened to new dangers on that day.

On that morning, the threats that had gathered far across the world appeared suddenly in our own cities. The world changed on that day. The enemies of the United States showed the harm they can do and the evil they intend. Since that September morning, our enemies have also seen something: they have seen the will and the might of the United States military, and they are meeting the fate they chose for themselves.

Our nation is waging a broad and unrelenting campaign against the global terror network, and we're winning. Wherever al Qaeda terrorists[1] try to hide, from the caves and mountains of Central Asia, to the islands of the Philippines, to the cities in Pakistan, we are finding them, and we are bringing them to justice.

Our nation is waging a broad and unrelenting campaign against the global terror network, and we're winning.

In the last two days, we captured a major terrorist, named Hambali. He's a known killer who was a close associate of September the 11th mastermind Khalid Shaykh Muhammad. Hambali was one of the world's most lethal terrorists who is suspected of planning major terrorist operations, including that which occurred in Bali, Indonesia, and other recent attacks. He is no longer a problem to those of us who love freedom, and neither are nearly two-thirds of known senior al Qaeda leaders, operational managers, and key facilitators who have been captured or have been killed.

Now, we're making progress. Slowly but surely, we're doing our duty to our fellow citizens. Now, al Qaeda is still active, and they're still recruiting, and they're still a threat because we won't cower. Its leaders and

---

1. Al Qaeda is the terrorist group that perpetrated the September 11, 2001, attacks on America. It is headed by terrorist mastermind Osama bin Laden.

foot soldiers continue to plot against the American people. But every terrorist can be certain of this: wherever they are, we will hunt them down one by one until they are no longer a threat to the people who live in the United States of America.

Progress in Afghanistan

Many of you served in [Afghanistan in 2001 during] Operation Enduring Freedom, and we thank you for your service. You can be proud of [your] help—to liberate the good people of Afghanistan from the thugs who turned that country into a training camp for al Qaeda terrorists. You enforced the doctrine which said, if you harbor a terrorist, if you hide a terrorist, if you feed a terrorist, you're just as guilty as the terrorists—and the Taliban [the toppled government of Afghanistan] found out what we meant.

Afghanistan today is a friend of the United States.

Afghanistan today is a friend of the United States of America. It is not a haven for America's terrorist enemies. As NATO [North Atlantic Treaty Organization] assumes a leading role in keeping Afghanistan secure, we're helping with the reconstruction and the founding of a democratic government. We're making steady progress in Afghanistan. New roads are being built, medical clinics are opening, there are new schools in Afghanistan where many young girls are now going to school for the first time, thanks to the United States of America.

We've also helped to build an Afghan national army. We want the Afghan people to defend themselves at some point in time. This army launched its first major operation, called Warrior Sweep, which are hunting down the terrorists, along with the help of the United States of America. Now thanks to the United States and our fine allies, Afghanistan is no longer a haven for terror, the Taliban is history, and the Afghan people are free.

Iraq has been liberated

The war on terror also continues in Iraq. Make no mistake about it, Iraq is part of the war on terror. Our coalition forces are still engaged in an essential mission. We met the major combat objectives in Operation Iraqi Freedom by removing a regime that persecuted Iraqis, and supported terrorists, and was armed to threaten the peace of the world. All the world is now seeing just how badly the Iraqi people suffered under this brutal dictator. The Iraqi people, themselves, are seeing a new day thanks to the brave men and women who came to liberate them.

Thanks to our military, Iraqi citizens do not have to fear a secret police, arbitrary arrests, or loved ones lost forever, and mass graves. Thanks to our military, the torture chambers of a dictator are closed, the prison cells for children are empty. Thanks to our military, Saddam Hussein will never threaten anybody with a weapon of mass destruction.

Many members of the former regime challenged our military and had their day of reckoning, and the other ones still in there have a lot to worry about. Parts of Iraq are still dangerous because freedom has enemies inside of Iraq. Men loyal to the fallen regime, some joined by foreign terrorists, are trying to prevent order and stability.

Rebuilding a free Iraq

We're on the offensive against these killers; we're going after them; we'll raid their hiding places; and we'll find them. The brave Americans who carry out these missions can know they will have every tool and every resource they need to defend themselves and to do the job they were sent to do. The terrorists will meet their end. And in the meantime, the Iraqi people are making steady progress, and building a stable society, and beginning to form a democratic government. Iraq's new Governing Council represents the nation's diverse groups.

> *A free and peaceful Iraq is an important part of winning the war on terror.*

In the months ahead, Iraqis will begin drafting a new constitution, and this will prepare the way for elections. America and our coalition are training Iraqi civil defense and police forces so they can patrol their own cities and their own villages. We're training a new army, an army that defends the people instead of terrorizes them.

Life is returning to normal for a lot of citizens in Iraq. Hospitals and universities have opened, in many places, water and other utility services are reaching pre-war levels. For the first time, a free press is operating in Iraq. Across Iraq, nearly all schoolchildren have completed their exams. And now, those children are receiving a real education without the hateful propaganda of Saddam Hussein.

By the hard efforts of our military, we are keeping our word to the world and to the Iraqi people. The illegal weapons hidden by the former regime will be found. The free and representative government Iraqis are building is there to stay.

A free and peaceful Iraq is an important part of winning the war on terror. A free Iraq will no longer be a training ground for terrorists, will no longer supply them with money or weapons. A free Iraq will help to rid the Middle East of resentment, and violence, and radicalism. A free Iraq will show all nations of the region that human freedom brings progress and prosperity. By working for peace and stability in the Middle East, we're making America, and future generations of Americans, more secure.

The United States is ready

Our actions in Iraq are part of a duty we have accepted across the world for keeping our resolve, and we will stay focused on the war on terror. The United States will not stand by and wait for another attack. We will not trust the restraint or good intentions of evil people. We will oppose terrorists and all who support them. We will not permit any terrorist group or outlaw regime to threaten us with weapons of mass destruction. And, when necessary, we will act decisively to protect the lives of our fellow citizens.

As our nation confronts great challenges, we rely, as always, on the goodness and courage of the men and women of our military. Like all our men and women who continue to serve in Iraq, you've done hard duty, far from home and family, and I know you'll never forget the people who fought at your side.

As a major from Miramar [Marine Corps air station in Southern California] said of his fellow Marines who served in Iraq, "They are my brothers and sisters." Each of you recalls especially the ones who gave their lives for freedom of others. The United States will always honor their memory. And, today, we ask the Almighty's blessings on those who grieve here on earth for their loved ones.

I know you're proud to wear the same uniform they wore. Each of you has chosen, you have made the choice, to fill a great calling, to live by a code of honor, in service to your nation, for the safety and security of your fellow citizens. You and I have taken an oath to defend America. We're meeting that duty together. And I am proud to be the Commander-in-Chief of such a fabulous group of men and women who wear our uniform. May God bless you.

May God bless you and your families. May God continue to bless the United States of America.

2

America Is Losing
the War on Terrorism

Karina Rollins

Karina Rollins is a senior editor at the American Enterprise.

The multifaceted war on terrorism is going badly. Domestic security is a joke; airline security is minimal and inefficient, while vulnerable sectors of the homeland, such as ports, factories, and power plants, remain completely unprotected. Police, firefighters, and emergency medical technicians are underfunded and disorganized, while members of the intelligence community still do not have key terror-fighting tools. The nation also continues to lack adequate defense against biological, chemical, and nuclear weapons. Furthermore, embarrassing bureaucratic blunders, such as granting visas to terrorists, undermine the war on terrorism. The Bush administration needs to address these glaring problems before any victory in the war on terrorism can be declared.

After 19 terrorists hijacked commercial airplanes, crashed them into the World Trade Center and the Pentagon, and killed over 3,000 Americans [on September 11, 2001], the U.S. government sprang into action: The director of the Federal Bureau of Investigation held a friendly meeting with an American Muslim group with known ties to terrorists. The State Department printed up thousands of copies of a poster series, "Mosques of America," and sponsored an imam-exchange program. None of which attracted any criticism from the attorney general or the President; all of which would be amusing if it were a sketch on [the television show] "Saturday Night Live."

The nation's new and improved airport security is a joke; all the stories about little blue-haired ladies' shoes searched for explosives are true. Americans know the hassle and make-work and plastic forks don't add to their safety. One of the biggest laugh lines of Washington, D.C.'s political comedy troupe, The Capitol Steps, comes at the beginning of a skit about airport security. A man in a giant turban walks on stage and hangs a big sign that reads simply, "O'Hare Security." It brings down the house.

Karina Rollins, "No Compromises: Why We Are Going to Lose the War on Terror . . . and How We Could Win," *The American Enterprise*, vol. 14, January/February 2003, p. 18. Copyright © 2003 by the American Enterprise Institute for Public Policy Research. Reproduced by permission of *The American Enterprise*, a magazine of Politics, Business, and Culture. On the Web at www.TAEmag.com.

Former senators Warren Rudman and Gary Hart, co-chairmen of the Commission on National Security in the 21st Century, concluded that "A year after [the terrorist attacks of September 11, 2001], America remains dangerously unprepared to prevent and respond to a catastrophic terrorist attack on U.S. soil." Rudman and Hart lament that enormous amounts of money are spent on airports, while port and cargo security take a back seat; that police, firemen, and emergency medical workers still can't communicate well with each other or their counterparts in nearby cities; that public health facilities are unprepared for a biological or chemical attack; that local police work in an intelligence vacuum and don't have access to terrorist watch lists; and that there has been no national debate about how to protect factories and power plants. Cyberspace is still glaringly unprotected as well.

"America remains dangerously unprepared to prevent and respond to a catastrophic terrorist attack on U.S. soil."

The Homeland Security bill has now, after many distractions, finally been passed. It will be the job of the new department to close the gaping security holes, and it will surely be successful in implementing some effective safety mechanisms. But it could take years for the department to become operational. Besides, addressing such practical matters is only half the solution; there is an entire worldview in Washington that must change drastically.

The administration publicly characterizes [the terrorist network] al-Qaeda and its sympathizers as a group of criminals, ignoring the religious nature of their plans to destroy the West. If the government—and the American people—are to win the war on terror, both must understand that our enemies have succeeded in launching a holy war—a war that will most certainly last beyond the lifetime of anyone reading these pages.

More than a year after [September 11], too many clear and present dangers continue to loom over Americans. Following are prescriptions to address some of the biggest problems:

Return to common sense and purge political correctness

Transportation Secretary Norman Mineta frets that being more suspicious of Arab males than 12-year-old girls will lead to World War II–style internment camps for Muslims.[1] When asked several months ago on [the television news program] "60 Minutes" if elderly white women and young Muslim men should be treated the same at the airport security gate, he answered "Basically, I would hope so." The President praises Mr. Mineta for outstanding performance.

---

1. During World War II, the U.S. government rounded up people of Japanese descent, citizens and noncitizens, and placed them in internment camps for the duration of the war. In later years, the internment of the Japanese was widely criticized for being discriminatory, unjust, and paranoid. The experience has been cited as a reason why profiling or other types of ethnic targeting should not be pursued in the name of security.

As William Lind of the Free Congress Foundation realizes, "The same government that wants to invade Iraq is too intimidated by political correctness to provide homeland security by profiling terrorists. The government's feeble efforts to protect our own perimeter spread fear and erode loyalties by telling patriotic citizens that their own government does not or cannot differentiate between patriots and terrorists." In a small bit of encouraging news, the government has announced plans to fingerprint and photograph men who are citizens of countries on an adjustable terror watch list. No, racial profiling isn't the answer. But terrorist profiling is. And that means being wary of young Arab-looking men. It's reality.

Eliminate terrorist training camps—for real

The United States "should immediately tell all nations that have terrorist training camps on their territory that they should get rid of them," declares Cliff May, president of the Foundation for the Defense of Democracies. "We should tell these countries we would like them to take care of the camps on their own. If they don't, we should tell them: 'We are going to violate your sovereignty to eliminate them if you do not.' We should give them a limited amount of time. If they don't comply, we should have contingency plans to eliminate the camps through bombing or commando raids.

More than a year after [September 11], too many clear and present dangers continue to loom over Americans.

"There is a lot of talk about the recruitment of terrorists, but you can't become a terrorist unless you're trained to be one. You need training to become a sniper or a suicide bomber. You have to go someplace where they teach you. It is vital that there be no such places in the world within the next six months."

Give security clearances to local police and plan statewide responses

"What's important is trust and inclusion," says Edward Davis, police superintendent of Lowell, Massachusetts. "That only happens through face-to-face contact. It's important that local police have security clearances. I have one and it makes me feel like I'm in the game. The joint task forces are working pretty well here in Massachusetts.

"And there has to be more discussion of regional responses to incidents. Jurisdictional issues have to be ironed out. There should be response scenarios that are clear, that can be trained, and that take care of the communications and coordination problems that can happen. If I had 1,000 police officers here tomorrow, I wouldn't really know how to coordinate them. You need a plan in advance. Not a complicated one, but a plan nonetheless. We need to do a better job planning for responses on a statewide level."

Issue national I.D. cards

National I.D. cards are a scary thought for many Americans, conjuring up images of Big Brother and George Orwell's dystopia.[2] Enough with the hysteria already. "Like it or not," points out my colleague Eli Lehrer, who founded the Heritage Foundation's Excellence in Policing Project and has written extensively about national identity cards, "Americans already have national I.D. cards. When they travel overseas, open a bank account, start a new job, or buy a gun, U.S. citizens need to provide state-issued identification. A citizen who gets stopped by the police and can't produce a driver's license, passport, or Social Security card will often have to spend the night in jail." It's hard to argue that this constitutes government power run amok.

A national I.D. card, far from robbing Americans of freedom or privacy, would simply make it much easier for police to tell the majority of law-abiding people from the small proportion of criminals and terrorists in our midst who are capable of doing real harm. It would make us safer—and that makes us freer.

Stop pretending that Saudi Arabia is our friend

As former assistant secretary of defense Frank Gaffney, Jr., now president of the Center for Security Policy, explains: "Saudi Arabia's alignment with America's enemies extends far beyond the anti-U.S. and anti-Western propaganda that is also ceaselessly disseminated by the kingdom's government-run media. For some fifty years, Saudi officials, royal family, and what passes for private sector institutions have been expending untold sums to promote the state religion—a virulently intolerant strain of Islam known as Wahabism. Washington has long ignored the individual and cumulative effects of such spending on Wahabi proselytizing, recruiting, indoctrination, training, and equipping of adherents who embrace the sect's injunction to convert or kill infidels.

"In the wake of terrorism made possible—or at least abetted—at home and abroad by such Saudi-connected activities, the United States can no longer afford to turn a blind eye to this profoundly unfriendly behavior. That is particularly true insofar as there is reason to believe that Wahabi enterprises are giving rise to perhaps the most insidious enemy of all: an Islamist Fifth Column operating within this country."

As of the printing of this [viewpoint], the White House continues to call the Saudis "good partners" in the war on terror.

Pray that the State Department doesn't destroy us

The State Department is directly responsible for issuing visas to the 19 September 11 hijackers, almost all of which should have been flatly rejected. The consular officers who issued the visas each received bonuses of $10,000 to $15,000. The State Department's Visa Express program, which let Saudi citizens apply for visas at Saudi travel agencies and pro-

---

2. In his famous work *1984*, author George Orwell wrote of a society in which all citizens were thoroughly spied on and privacy did not exist.

vided even fewer safeguards than the regular system, continued for almost a whole year after [September 11].

The Homeland Security Act includes stricter visa controls for Saudi citizens—but only by accident. If the State Department had had its way, those controls would have been wiped clear off the bill: State objected to the singling out of Saudi Arabia—the country from which came 15 of the 19 September 11 hijackers. Joel Mowbray, who first broke the visa scandal story in *National Review*, reports that the department was assured, incredibly, that the Saudi provision would be struck from the legislation. Only due to "the last-minute confusion and the rush to get the mammoth bill passed . . ." he says, did the provision stay put.

> *The State Department is directly responsible for issuing visas to the 19 September 11 hijackers, almost all of which should have been flatly rejected.*

Unfazed by even the most egregious breaches of security, Secretary of State Colin Powell continues to wax poetic: "From the mountains of Afghanistan to the valleys of Bosnia to the plains of Africa to the forests of Asia and around the world we are on the ground working with our Muslim partners to expand to the circle of peace, the circle of prosperity, the circle of freedom."

Secretary Powell also wants more of these "partners" on the ground right here in the U.S., pledging to expand programs to bring more Islamic political and religious leaders as well as journalists and teachers to America.

Get serious about border control and immigration

The Immigration and Naturalization Service is guilty of the same reckless sloppiness in approving documents as the State Department. Of course, the INS is also understaffed and underfunded—something which could start to be fixed immediately (and should have been started on September 12, 2001). The administration seems to lack any real sense of urgency about the country's porous borders, and the lack of cooperation from our Mexican and, especially, Canadian neighbors.

"When it comes to immigration, the President's approach is guided by compassion and fairness," says Sharon Castillo, a spokesman for the Republican National Committee. No word on how fair it is to Americans who died at the hands of terrorists who could have been kept out of the country.

Recognize the threat in our midst

Terror expert Steven Emerson founded The Investigative Project to collect data on militant Muslim groups in the U.S. In his book *American Jihad: The Terrorists Living Among Us*, he points to nine "terrorist support networks" based in America: Muslim Arab Youth Association, the American Islamic Group, Islamic Cultural Workshop, the Council on American-Islamic Relations, the American Muslim Council, Islamic Circle of North

America, the Muslim Public Affairs Council, the American Muslim Alliance, and the Islamic Society of North America.

These groups, Emerson says, use "the laws, freedoms, and loopholes of the most liberal nation on earth to help finance and direct one of the most violent international terrorism groups in the world." "Operating in the free-wheeling and tolerant environment of the United States, bin Laden was able to set up a whole array of 'cells' in a loosely organized network that included Tucson, Arizona; Brooklyn, New York; Orlando, Florida; Dallas, Texas; Santa Clara, California; Columbia, Missouri; and Herndon, Virginia."

Start pointing fingers

No reform or security measure is going to mean very much if the people who egregiously violate the most basic rules, and those in charge of them, aren't held accountable, which in most cases means being fired. After [September 11], the administration and members of Congress bent over backwards to insist that no one was finger pointing or seeking to lay blame. But accountability is precisely what's needed.

Minneapolis FBI special agent Coleen Rowley and her team did everything in their power to get authorization from FBI headquarters merely to search the computer of Zacarias Moussaoui, the so-called twentieth hijacker. They were stalled and denied at every turn, despite providing clear evidence for the necessity of the search. One supervisory special agent in particular was responsible for the travesty. FBI Director Robert Mueller's response when Rowley's memo[3] made the front pages: announcing plans to hire more agents and buy new computers. Oh, and he promoted that supervisory agent.

Calling for Mueller's resignation back in May, the *Wall Street Journal* pointed out the obvious: "If Mueller had wanted to send a message to change the FBI mindset he would have fired the supervisory special agent who ignored the Minneapolis warnings on Moussaoui." To make matters worse, Mueller and Attorney General John Ashcroft did not inform the President of the debacle for seven months. As long as Robert Mueller is allowed to keep his job, the FBI's credibility is nonexistent. The White House's response: praise all around.

So, how safe are we?

3. In May 2002 Agent Rowley wrote a memo to the head of the FBI expressing concerns that the FBI had ignored evidence that was available prior to September 11, 2001, indicating that an attack may be in the works.

3

A War on Terrorism Is Futile

Michael Massing

Michael Massing is the author of The Fix, *a critical study of the war on drugs. His work has also appeared in the* Nation *and on* Alternet. *He is the former executive editor of* Columbia Journalism Review.

If the war on terrorism is modeled on the war on drugs—a continual battle against an elusive and changing enemy—it will be an ongoing failure. A military response to terrorism will only create more terrorism. Targeting specific terrorists is also not a permanent solution, as more will simply spring up to replace those removed. Instead of a war on terrorism, the United States should focus on preventing terrorist attacks on the homeland. This approach would be safer and more effective than becoming entangled in unstable, hostile countries around the world. To overcome the inefficiencies of existing federal agencies, a Terrorism Prevention Agency should be established that would focus solely on domestic antiterrorism efforts.

"This is a different kind of conflict," said General Richard B. Myers, chairman of the Joint Chiefs of Staff, at a Pentagon briefing in October [2001]. He was speaking of the war on terrorism. "The closest analogy would be the drug war." Since September 11 [2001, when terrorists attacked the United States], comparisons between the two wars have been rife: Both are said to involve an elusive and resourceful enemy capable of inflicting tremendous damage on the United States; both are cast as a long, drawn-out struggle that requires concentrated efforts on multiple fronts; and both are led by a powerful "czar" authorized to knock heads, challenge budgets, and mobilize resources.

Heaven help us. The war on drugs has been a dismal failure. Every year, the federal government spends almost $20 billion to fight illicit drugs. It has tracked planes in Peru, sent helicopters to Colombia, installed X-ray machines along the Mexican border, and sent AWACS [Airborne Warning and Control System] surveillance planes over the Caribbean. Yet drugs continue to pour into [the United States]. Cocaine today sells at record-low prices and heroin is available at record-high purity levels. And despite the 1.5 million drug arrests made every year and the

400,000 drug offenders now in prison, the level of addiction in the United States remains stubbornly high. So to the extent that the war on terrorism emulates the war on drugs, we're in big trouble.

Is there another way? Over the past 10 years, I've studied the drug war on various fronts: from the coca fields of the Andes to the smuggling zones along the Mexican border to the drug-ridden neighborhoods of New York and Washington, D.C. And that experience leads me to believe that the war on drugs offers valuable lessons on how—and how not—to fight the war on terrorism.

Attack the roots of terrorism, not the symptoms

Consider, for instance, the idea that in fighting terrorism we should focus on its "root causes." Such an approach was succinctly described by Philip Wilcox, Jr., the U.S. ambassador at large for counterterrorism from 1994 to 1997, in the October 18 *New York Review of Books*. To respond to the attacks on the World Trade Center and the Pentagon with military force, Wilcox asserted, would simply generate more terrorism. Instead, he wrote, the United States should adopt a foreign policy that "deals not just with the symptoms but with the roots of terrorism, broadly defined." America, Wilcox continued, should seek to moderate the "conditions that breed violence and terrorism" through efforts to "resolve conflicts"—especially the one between Israelis and Palestinians—and through "assistance for economic development, education, and population control."

A similar case has frequently been made with respect to both the production and consumption of drugs. The world's poor, who cultivate drugs for export, need better economic opportunities. And to reduce the level of drug abuse in America, we need to address the socioeconomic conditions that generate it. Studies suggest that drug abuse is especially prevalent in disadvantaged communities and that programs to create jobs, provide housing, and raise the minimum wage could help shrink the pool of potential addicts. Clearly, though, such programs would take many years to bear fruit. In the meantime, drug abuse—and all its attendant harms—would flourish.

To the extent that the war on terrorism emulates the war on drugs, we're in big trouble.

So, too, with terror. America does need to address the poverty and desperation that fuel the fires of Islamic fundamentalism, just as it must overcome the foreign-policy legacy that makes the United States a target. Yet solutions to these problems may take decades to unfold—and in the interim, the Osama bin Ladens of the world would be free to wreak their havoc. In the short run, a more direct antidote is needed.

The CIA and covert tactics

For some, that antidote is "going to the source" of the problem. Here, too, there are clear echoes of the drug war. In the case of terrorism, the most immediate source, of course, is bin Laden and al-Qaeda. But as President [George W.] Bush has said, the war on terror "will not end until every terrorist group of global reach has been found, stopped, and defeated." And there has been general agreement that a revived Central Intelligence Agency should be a principal policy instrument. The agency's ability to gather intelligence and to carry out covert operations, it's said, makes it an ideal institution to combat terrorism. Writing in *The Wall Street Journal*, Herbert E. Meyer, a senior CIA official during the Reagan years, decried the agency's recent passivity and urged it to become more aggressive, as it was under William Casey, his former boss. "We smuggled weapons to freedom fighters throughout the world, we smuggled bibles into the Soviet Union itself, and we mined harbors in Nicaragua," Meyer wrote. Such tactics, he asserted, helped to bring about the collapse of communism and could vanquish terrorism, too.

The war on drugs offers valuable lessons on how—and how not—to fight the war on terrorism.

David Ignatius, in a *Washington Post* column, praised the CIA's Counter-Terrorism Center in Langley, Virginia, for its covert capability "ranging from paramilitary operations to the sort of dirty tricks and political subversion that can overthrow governments supporting terrorism." Even Seymour Hersh, who has written so extensively about U.S. misadventures abroad, blamed the U.S. government's failure to detect September 11 largely on a weakened CIA. Ruing a 1995 directive that discouraged the use of recruits with unsavory records, Hersh wrote in *The New Yorker* that "hundreds of 'assets' were indiscriminately stricken from the CIA's payroll, with a devastating effect on anti-terrorist operations in the Middle East." In recent years, an unnamed senior general told him, "we've been hiring kids out of college who are computer geeks. This is about going back to deep, hard dirty work, with tough people going down dark alleys with good instincts."

According to the *Post*, the administration has already added more than $1 billion to the CIA's antiterrorism budget—much of it for new covert actions, including the killing of specified individuals. "The gloves are off," one senior official told [reporter] Bob Woodward. "The president has given the agency the green light to do whatever is necessary. Lethal operations that were unthinkable pre–September 11 are now underway."

There is no shortage of terrorists

For those of us who have covered the drug war, this also sounds depressingly familiar. For nearly three decades, the United States has attempted to fight drugs by attacking them at their "source": the countries that cultivate, produce, and smuggle them. Leading this effort has been the Drug Enforcement Administration [DEA]. In the mid-1980s, the DEA's main target was Pablo Escobar and the Medellin cartel; together, they were said to control as much as 80 percent of the cocaine entering the United States. In 1993, after years of wiretaps, spying, and raids, the Colombians, helped by U.S. operatives, finally managed to corner and kill Escobar. And the Medellin cartel disintegrated along with him.

Their demise did produce some short-term benefits. In the world of Colombian drug traffickers, Escobar stood out for his brutality, and his death led to a temporary fall-off in the number of car bombs and political assassinations. Yet the vacuum left by the Medellin cartel was quickly filled by the rival Cali cartel. So the DEA went after it. In a few years, it, too, was destroyed—and quickly replaced by a host of smaller but no less efficient syndicates. What's more, the campaign against the Colombian cartels created an opening for Mexico's drug traffickers, who, newly enriched, formed violent syndicates along America's southern border. Meanwhile, cocaine kept cascading into the United States.

A similar result seems likely in the war on terrorism. The campaign against al-Qaeda and the Taliban [the former rulers of Afghanistan] may be necessary as an act of self-defense. But thousands of young fanatics throughout the Arab world are eager to become martyrs, and every terrorist who's hunted down and killed is likely to be replaced by others. Indeed, the covert actions undertaken against terrorist cells abroad could themselves generate new recruits for the cause.

The CIA cannot get to the sources of terrorism

Furthermore, there's a limit to what the CIA can realistically achieve. It's not easy for Americans to work undercover in the Middle East. And it's nearly impossible for them to penetrate terrorist cells. In *The Atlantic Monthly* . . . , Reuel Marc Gerecht, who for nearly nine years worked for the CIA on Middle Eastern matters, described what it was like to walk through the Afghan neighborhoods of Peshawar, Pakistan, where bin Laden does much of his recruiting.

> Even in the darkness I had a case officer's worst sensation— eyes following me everywhere. To escape the crowds I would pop into carpet, copper, and jewelry shops. . . . No matter where I went, the feeling never left me. I couldn't see how the CIA as it is today had any chance of running a successful counterterrorist operation against bin Laden in Peshawar, the Dodge City of Central Asia.

More generally, Gerecht went on,

> Westerners cannot visit the cinder-block, mud-brick side of the Muslim world—whence bin Laden's foot soldiers mostly come—without announcing who they are. No case officer stationed in Pakistan can penetrate either the Afghan communities in Peshawar or the Northwest Frontier's numerous religious schools, which feed manpower and ideas to bin Laden and the Taliban, and seriously expect to gather information about radical Islamic terrorism—let alone recruit foreign agents.

Add in the CIA's much-publicized dearth of agents who know the Middle East and speak its languages and it's clear that the agency is many years away from making any real inroads into the terrorist underworld.

What's more, unleashing the CIA could have many dire side effects. Just look at its past: From the Congo, where the agency helped to assassinate Prime Minister Patrice Lumumba, to Chile, where it helped to overthrow President Salvador Allende, to Central America, where it worked with death squads, America's covert operations often were ugly and often produced backlash. Our current troubles in Afghanistan are partly an unintended consequence of the CIA's secret program to arm the mujahideen there. Even with a worthy goal like quashing terrorism, freeing the CIA to play dirty again seems likely to backfire.

If addressing the root causes of terrorism seems too vague and drawn-out a solution, and if going to the source seems too difficult and dangerous, what is to be done? Is there no alternative that offers more promise?

Domestic prevention is the best strategy

In fact, there is one—and the war on drugs can help point the way. My research on drugs suggests that of all the ways to reduce drug abuse in America, one stands out: cutting the demand for drugs through treatment. Where terrorism is concerned, however, there is no equivalent of demand or of treatment to reduce it. Any solution must take place on the supply side.

Here, too, there is a drug analogy. From watching police actions on a drug-infested block in East Harlem and from interviewing police officers, drug-enforcement agents, and drug traffickers, I concluded that domestic law enforcement represents the best way to combat the drug trade. Far more than stalking traffickers in Colombia or seizing drugs at the border, collaring dealers on the street and dismantling local drug gangs seemed to reduce the crime associated with drugs and to restore a sense of neighborhood safety. Mayor Rudy Giuliani's campaign to squash drug dealing in New York City has in many ways been shortsighted, for it has not been accompanied by a parallel campaign to reduce the demand for drugs; but I have grudgingly come to believe that it has eliminated some of the more egregious aspects of the city's drug trade. All in all, the closer enforcement gets to the point where drugs do the most harm—the street—the more impact it seems to have. . . .

> *Thousands of young fanatics throughout the Arab world are eager to become martyrs, and every terrorist who's hunted down and killed is likely to be replaced by others.*

Might not the same be true with terrorism? . . . If our main goal is to prevent future terrorist attacks, wouldn't it be more effective to concentrate our enforcement efforts here, in the United States, instead of operating on the hostile terrain of the Middle East? In all the talk about unleashing the CIA, it's often overlooked that the perpetrators of September 11 had been living in this country for years. In detecting and rooting out terrorists, shouldn't we tend primarily to our own backyard?

Emphasizing prevention at home would offer a number of advantages.

First, it's much easier to carry out undercover work here than abroad. Agents face fewer hazards in San Diego, Trenton, and Boca Raton than they do in Beirut, Cairo, or Peshawar. And we have many more resources here. In addition to the FBI and other federal agencies, thousands of local police officers are working on terrorism in cities across the country. In the drug war, the local police have led the way in dismantling drug gangs, and they could make a similar contribution toward uprooting terrorist networks. Furthermore, when it comes to obtaining "HUMINT"—the critical "human intelligence" collected by investigative agencies—the millions of loyal American Muslims living in this country would seem a far more fruitful source than Islamic fundamentalists in the Middle East. Finally, concentrating on domestic law enforcement would avoid the types of covert actions that have proved so costly and embarrassing in the past.

It's often overlooked that the perpetrators of September 11 had been living in this country for years. . . . Shouldn't we tend primarily to our own backyard?

This is not to say that foreign intelligence gathering has no role. Jim Dempsey, an analyst at the Center for Democracy and Technology in Washington, D.C., who previously monitored the FBI for the House Judiciary Committee, observes that the FBI receives hundreds of tips every day about possible terrorists and that it's impossible to sift through them all. In the case of the September 11 hijackers, he notes, "nothing they did in the United States brought them to the attention of U.S. agencies." To make sense of all the information flowing into the FBI, Dempsey says, the bureau needs leads from abroad: "Through either electronic or human sources or through liaison relations with foreign services, you develop overseas the information that says that so-and-so is coming to the United States."

Existing agencies are not ideal

Needless to say, a domestic antiterrorism strategy would raise some concerns. "Unleashing" the FBI, for instance, could lead the bureau to engage in the same type of domestic spying that so marred the tenure of [former FBI director] J. Edgar Hoover. Although the federal government does need expanded powers in this new era, the potential for abuse of civil liberties is clear. Any domestic crackdown, then, would have to be accompanied by vigilant oversight.

Another problem is the culture of the FBI. . . . The bureau's reluctance to share information with other federal agencies and with local authorities has hindered many investigations. In the first case of anthrax to hit New York City, at NBC, the FBI did not immediately inform the city about the letter that was thought to be suspicious—an oversight that infuriated Mayor Giuliani. At a congressional hearing in late October [2001], Giuliani called for legislation that would increase the sharing of information between federal and local law-enforcement agencies.

Such bureaucratic fragmentation has generated fresh ideas about new institutional arrangements for fighting terrorism. Despite their qualms about the new police powers legislated in the name of antiterrorism, even some civil libertarians support consolidating federal intelligence efforts in a single agency. Morton Halperin, a longtime leader of the American Civil Liberties Union, told an October 16 forum sponsored by *The American Prospect* that he favored creation of one agency that would be both more effective and more accountable.

Jack Riley, a counterterrorism specialist at the Rand Corporation, adds that "when you start looking at where the gaps are in U.S. efforts to fight terrorism, they are probably easier to fill here than overseas." The CIA could still supply the FBI with foreign intelligence. As long as the two agencies continue to function separately, however, it's hard for them to piece together a comprehensive picture of how terrorists operate both here and abroad and coordinate forces to confront them.

A terrorism prevention agency

What is needed, Riley says, is a seamless new organization that brings together counterterrorism specialists from these two institutions as well as from other federal organizations. Investigators, intelligence analysts, financial wizards, customs specialists, communications whizzes, immigration experts, liaisons to foreign and local police departments—they all need to be joined together in a new agency with one overarching goal: preventing future terrorist attacks in the United States. In the end, Riley adds, we need "a terrorism equivalent of the DEA."

My initial reaction on hearing this was to shudder. For in fighting the drug war, the DEA has been singularly ineffectual. Despite the huge increases in its budget and staff over the past 20 years, it has failed in its mission to reduce the supply of outlawed drugs in this country. That's because the drug problem in America is at heart a public-health problem—one that no amount of arrest and prosecution can contain.

But terrorism is different. It's a highly lethal threat directed by calculating criminals at America's very core, and it must be confronted with every available weapon. The new Office of Homeland Security, whose duties seem to encompass everything from stocking smallpox vaccines to bolstering airport security, is too diffuse and weak to carry out the task at hand. For that, America needs an entirely new and independent body—a Terrorism Prevention Agency. And given the hopelessness of the war on drugs, frustrated agents from the DEA could be assigned to it. At a new TPA, they might actually be able to do some good.

4

Expanded Law Enforcement Powers Have Reduced Terrorism

John Ashcroft

John Ashcroft is the attorney general of the United States.

The greatest tribute Americans could pay those who died in the September 11, 2001, terrorist attacks would be to defend the United States and prevent future attacks from occurring. This cause has already been undertaken with the adoption of the USA PATRIOT Act, which expands government powers and intelligence capabilities in order to reduce terrorism. Since the Patriot Act was passed, authorities have made great strides in the war on terrorism, while preserving the safety and liberty of Americans.

Editor's Note: The following were prepared remarks given at the American Enterprise Institute in Washington, D.C., on August 19, 2003.

This morning [August 19, 2003], terrorists struck the United Nations mission in Baghdad, killing at least 13 people and seriously injuring at least 120 others. The victims were innocent people who traveled to Iraq on a mission of peace and human dignity. Let me express sympathy to the victims and their loved ones.

This morning's attack again confirms that the worldwide terrorist threat is real and imminent. Our enemies continue to pursue ways to murder the innocent and the peaceful. They seek to kill us abroad and at home. But we will not be deterred from our responsibility to preserve American life and liberty, nor our duty to build a safer, more secure world.

Memorials and warnings

Nearly two years have now passed since [September 11, 2001, when] American ground was hallowed by the blood of innocents.

John Ashcroft, address to the American Enterprise Institute, Washington, DC, August 19, 2003.

Two years separate us from the day when our nation's stock of consecrated ground grew tragically larger. That day, a familiar list of monuments to American freedom—places like Bunker Hill, Antietam, the Argonne, Iwo Jima, and Normandy Beach—grew longer by three:

16 acres in lower Manhattan.
The Pentagon.
A field in Shanksville, Pennsylvania.

For the dead, the hallowed spaces of freedom are memorials, testaments to their sacrifice. For the living, they are a warning. They are a reminder that the first responsibility of government is to provide the security that preserves the lives and liberty of the people.

In 1863, Abraham Lincoln stood on the hallowed ground of freedom at Gettysburg and expressed the sense of resolution familiar to anyone who has looked into the void at Ground Zero [at the site of the World Trade Center], surveyed the wreckage of the Pentagon, or seen the gash in the earth left by Flight 93.

Our final tribute to the dead of September 11th must be to fulfill our responsibility to defend the living.

"We cannot dedicate, we cannot consecrate, we cannot hallow this ground," Lincoln said. "The brave men, living and dead, who struggled here have consecrated it far above our poor power to add or detract."

The responsibility of those who remain, said Lincoln, is to honor the dead not with their words but with their actions—to be, quote, "dedicated to the unfinished work which they who fought here have thus far so nobly advanced."

The work of the living

It is now as it was then. We should build monuments. We should erect memorials. But our final tribute to the dead of September 11th must be to fulfill our responsibility to defend the living. Our greatest memorial to those who have passed must be to protect the lives and liberties of those yet to come.

The unfinished work of September 11 began before the towers fell, when Americans began to fight back against terror.

It was the work of the passengers on Flight 93, who fought to end the flight in a Pennsylvania field rather than a building on Pennsylvania Avenue.

It was the work of the fire fighters and police officers running up the stairs as others were running down.

It was the work of unknown heroes, whose stories will never be known, but whose spirit is the measure of hope we take from that terrible day.

The cause for which these men and women gave the last full measure of devotion—the protection of the lives and liberty of their fellow Americans—has become the cause of our time. It has transformed the mission of the Justice Department. In its service, the men and women of justice have given new meaning to sacrifice, and new depth to duty.

"Give us the tools and we will finish the job"

Where a culture of law enforcement inhibition prevented communication and coordination, we have built a new ethos of justice, one rooted in cooperation, nurtured by coordination, and focused on a single, overarching goal: the prevention of terrorist attacks. All of this has been done within the safeguards of our Constitution and its guarantees of protection for American freedom.

When terrorists had bested us with technology, communications, and information, we fought for the tools necessary to preserve the lives and liberty of the American people.

In the long winter of 1941, [former British prime minister] Winston Churchill appealed to the United States for help in defending freedom from Nazism with the phrase, "Give us the tools and we will finish the job." In the days after September 11, we appealed to Congress for help in defending freedom from terrorism with the same refrain: "Give us the tools and we will finish the job."

Congress responded by passing the USA Patriot Act by an overwhelming margin. And while our job is not finished, we have used the tools provided in the Patriot Act to fulfill our first responsibility to protect the American people. We have used these tools to prevent terrorists from unleashing more death and destruction on our soil. We have used these tools to save innocent American lives. *We have used these tools to provide the security that ensures liberty.*

Today, almost two years from the day of the attack, we know more than ever before about our capacity to defend ourselves from terrorists. We know now that there were fatal flaws in our national defenses prior to September 11. We know now that al Qaeda [the terrorist group that attacked America on September 11, 2001] understood these flaws. And we know now that al Qaeda exploited the flaws in our defenses to murderous effect.

Two years later, the evidence is clear: If we knew then what we know now, we would have passed the Patriot Act six months *before* September 11th rather than six weeks after the attacks.

For Congress to have done less would have been a failure of government's most basic responsibility to the American people . . . to preserve life and liberty.

For Congress to have done less would have ignored the lethal lessons taught that tragic day in September.

Increased communication

Congress recently completed an 18-month study of the causes of September 11th. Congress's conclusions—that there was a need for better communication, a need for better cooperation, a need for prevention—read like a preamble to the Patriot Act written two years after the hard lessons of history.

First, the report found that prior to September 11th intelligence agencies and law enforcement failed to communicate with each other about terrorist hijackers—even those identified as suspects. This lack of communications had its roots deep in the culture of government. The walls between those who gather intelligence and those who enforce the laws prevented action that could save lives.

Fortunately, in the Patriot Act, Congress began to tear down the walls that cut off communication between intelligence and law enforcement officials. The Patriot Act gave agencies like the FBI and the CIA the ability to integrate their capabilities. It gave government the ability to "connect the dots," revealing the shadowy terrorist network in our midst.

We have used the tools provided in the Patriot Act to fulfill our first responsibility to protect the American people.

In Portland, Oregon, we have indicted several persons for allegedly conspiring to travel to Afghanistan after the September 11th attacks in an effort to fight against American forces.[1] In an example of excellent information-sharing between local, state, and federal authorities, the investigation began when a local sheriff in another state shared with the Portland Joint Terrorism Task Force information one of his deputies had developed from a traffic stop.

Because the investigation involved both intelligence techniques and law enforcement tools, the Patriot Act's elimination of the "wall" was critical in allowing all of the dots to be connected and the criminal charges to be fully developed. Recently one of the defendants, Maher Hawash, pled guilty to illegally providing support to the Taliban and agreed to cooperate with the government. He faces a sentence of seven to ten years in prison.

Improved technology

Second, the congressional report on September 11th found that U.S. law enforcement had long been forced to rely on outdated and insufficient technology in its efforts to prevent terrorist attacks.

Fortunately, in the Patriot Act, Congress gave law enforcement improved tools to prevent terrorism in the age of high technology. For example, where before investigators were forced to get a different wiretap order every time a suspect changed cell phones, now investigators can get a single wiretap that applies to the suspect and various phones he uses.

Thanks to the Patriot Act, we may deploy technology to track and develop cases against alleged terrorist operatives.

Uzir Paracha was a Pakistani national living in New York, who allegedly met an al Qaeda operative overseas. Paracha allegedly agreed to help procure United States immigration documents, deposit money in a U.S. bank account, and use a post office box, all to allegedly facilitate the al Qaeda operative's clandestine arrival in this country.

---

1. American forces fought in Afghanistan in late 2001 to oust the Taliban government, which had given shelter to terrorist mastermind Osama bin Laden and his group al Qaeda.

Paracha was charged on August 8 with conspiracy to provide material support to al Qaeda.

Streamlined agencies

Third, the congressional report on September 11th determined that there was not enough cooperation among federal, state, and local law enforcement to combat a terrorist threat that found safe haven in the most nondescript of communities.

Fortunately, the Patriot Act expanded the capabilities of our Joint Terrorism Task Forces, which combine federal, state and local law enforcement officers into a seamless anti-terror team with international law enforcement and intelligence agencies.

Hemant Lakhani is an alleged arms dealer in Great Britain, who is charged with attempting to sell shoulder-fired missiles to terrorists for use against American targets. After a long undercover investigation in several countries, Lakhani traveled to Newark, New Jersey, last week, and was arrested, along with two alleged financial facilitators, as he allegedly prepared to finalize the sale of the first missile.

To abandon [the Patriot Act] would senselessly imperil American lives and American liberty, and ignore the lessons of September 11th.

The Lakhani investigation would not have been possible had American, Russian and other foreign intelligence and law enforcement agencies not been able to coordinate and communicate the intelligence they had gained from various investigative tools. . . .

Armed with the tools provided by the Patriot Act, the men and women of justice and law enforcement have dedicated themselves to the unfinished work of those who resisted, those who assisted, and those who sacrificed on September 11th.

Our efforts to reduce terrorism have been successful

We have neutralized alleged terrorist cells in Buffalo, Detroit, Seattle and Portland.

To date, we have brought 255 criminal charges. One hundred thirty two individuals have been convicted or pled guilty.

All told, more than 3,000 suspected terrorists have been arrested in many countries. Many more have met a different fate.

We have worked hard, but we have not labored alone:

Our efforts have been supported by Republicans and Democrats in Congress.

Our efforts have been ratified by the courts in legal challenge after legal challenge.

Our efforts have been rewarded by the trust of the American people. A two to one majority of Americans believe the Patriot Act is a necessary and effective tool that protects liberty, because it targets terrorists. Ninety one percent of Americans understand that the Patriot Act has not affected their civil rights or the civil rights of their families.

Lessons learned

The painful lessons of September 11th remain touchstones, reminding us of government's responsibility to its people. Those lessons have directed us down a path that preserves life and liberty.

Almost two years after Americans fought in the skies over Shanksville, we know that communication works. The Patriot Act opened opportunities for information sharing. To abandon this tool would disconnect the dots, risk American lives and liberty, and reject September 11th's lessons.

Almost two years after Americans died at the Pentagon, we know that cooperation works. The Patriot Act creates teamwork at every level of law enforcement and intelligence. To block cooperation against terrorists would make our nation more vulnerable to attack and reject the teachings of September 11th.

Almost two years after Americans and the citizens of more than 80 other nations died at the World Trade Center we know that prevention works. The Patriot Act gives us the technological tools to anticipate, adapt and out-think our terrorist enemy. To abandon these tools would senselessly imperil American lives and American liberty, and ignore the lessons of September 11th.

America is safe and free

The cause we have chosen is just. The course we have chosen is constitutional. The course we have chosen is preserving lives. For two years Americans have been safe. Because we are safer, our liberties are more secure.

During the long days of Operation Enduring Freedom, the struggle against the Taliban in Afghanistan, it was reported that every morning military commanders read a list to their troops—the names of men and women who died on September 11.

By reciting the names of the dead, the commanders paid tribute to the words of Lincoln, spoken on another battlefield 140 years and half a world away. They are words of hope, and words of resolution. "That from these honored dead," said Lincoln, "we take increased devotion to that cause for which they gave the last full measure of devotion."

That cause is liberty; given a new birth at Gettysburg, and reborn once again in the struggle which history places before us today. We did not seek this struggle, but we embrace this cause.

Providence, which has bestowed on America the responsibility to lead the world in liberty, has also handed America a great trust: to provide the security that ensures liberty.

We accept this trust not with anger or arrogance but with belief. Belief that liberty is the greatest gift of our Creator. Belief that such liberty is the universal endowment of all humanity. Belief that as long as there is an America, liberty must not, will not, shall not perish from the earth.

Thank you. God bless you and God bless America.

5

Expanded Law Enforcement Powers Violate Civil Liberties

Nick Gillespie

Nick Gillespie is editor in chief of Reason, *a libertarian magazine.*

When Americans unquestioningly sacrifice their civil liberties for the promise of security, they dishonor those who died in the September 11, 2001, terrorist attacks. Enhanced law enforcement powers such as those granted by the USA PATRIOT Act limit civil liberties in the name of security but provide little safety, challenging what is inherently free and honorable about America. Any threat to civil liberties should be viewed with suspicion, for a free society is eroded not overnight but over time; already Americans have become accustomed to an unprecedented level of increased surveillance and scrutiny, and further restrictions are on the way.

Amid the mad, horrific carnage of [the September 11, 2001, terrorist attacks on America]—amid the planes screaming into office buildings and cornfields; amid the last-minute phone calls by doomed innocents to loved ones; amid the victims so desperate that they dove from the heights of the World Trade Center to the pavement below (what nightmare thoughts must have shot through their minds in that all too brief yet interminable fall to Ground Zero?); amid the billowing cloud of ash that smothered Manhattan and the rest of the country like a volcanic eruption of unmitigated human suffering; amid the heroism of plane passengers and firemen and cops and neighbors; amid the crush of steel and concrete and glass that flattened 220 stories into a pile barely 50 feet tall—amid the 3,000 deaths that day, something else died too.

Swapping freedom for security

By nightfall, it seemed, we had changed from a nation that placed a uniquely high value on privacy and freedom to one that embraced security and safety as first principles. Of *course* we swapped freedom for safety.

Nick Gillespie, "Freedom for Safety: An Old Trade—and a Useless One," *Reason*, vol. 34, October 2002, pp. 25–26. Copyright © 2002 by the Reason Foundation. Reproduced by permission.

Just look again at those people jumping from the twin towers to understand why 78 percent of respondents in a recent Gallup/University of Oklahoma poll favored trading civil liberties for "security" (and why 71 percent supported a national ID card too).[1] Never mind that the trade hasn't made us safer, or that it erodes the freedom that we say is precisely what the terrorists hate about us.

Within days of the attacks, Attorney General John Ashcroft pushed Congress to pass expansive anti-terrorism legislation that was a lawman's wish list (and not very different from the regular requests made by lawmen before 9/11). We *must*, implored the man who had redirected FBI efforts away from counterterrorism and back toward battling drugs and kiddie porn, make it easier for cops and feds and spies to get the drop on suspects, broaden the definition of and increase the penalties for money laundering, impose new restrictions on immigration, and on and on.

Amid the 3,000 deaths that day, something else died too.

On October 26, 2001, President George W. Bush signed the USA PATRIOT Act, an acronym for a law so ludicrously named that it sounds like [satirist] Thomas Pynchon parodying [dystopia author] George Orwell: the Uniting and Strengthening America by Providing Appropriate Tools Required to Intercept and Obstruct Terrorism Act. As the Electronic Frontier Foundation (EFF) and other critics noted, the legislation ran to 342 pages and made major changes to over a dozen statutes that had limited government surveillance of citizens. We can assume that many legislators and their staffers, in the time-honored tradition, didn't read the text before casting their votes. Likewise, it will be years, not just months, before the act's full implications are clear.

The USA PATRIOT Act is a synecdoche for the freedom-for-safety swap. Among many other things, it sanctioned roving wiretaps (which allow police to track individuals over different phones and computers) and spying on the Web browsers of people who are not even criminal suspects. It rewrote the definitions of terrorism and money laundering to include all sorts of lesser and wider-ranging offenses. More important, as EFF underscored, "In asking for these broad new powers, the government made no showing that the previous powers of law enforcement and intelligence agencies to spy on U.S. citizens were insufficient to allow them to investigate and prosecute acts of terrorism." Nothing that's emerged in the past year contradicts that early assessment.

"We're likely to experience more restrictions on personal freedom than has ever been the case in this country," pronounced Supreme Court Justice Sandra Day O'Connor last year after visiting Ground Zero. So we have, in ways large and small, profound and trivial. The worst part of the

---

1. It has been proposed that the United States issue national ID cards to its citizens that would contain information such as a person's name, photo, address, and fingerprint. This is a controversial plan, criticized for making private information vulnerable to scrutiny without adding protection to Americans.

freedom-for-safety swap is that it's *never* a done deal; the safety providers are endless hagglers, always coming back for more. This fall's [2002] major homeland security legislation, unfinished at press time, will doubtless renew the negotiations.

Who knows where it will end? Freedom and privacy rarely, if ever, disappear in one fell swoop. In just a year, we've become accustomed to unnamed "detainees" being held in secret by the Department of Justice (and to the DOJ refusing to comply with state and federal court rulings to release the names of suspects); to the possibility of equally secret "military tribunals" (it's all right—they won't be used against U.S. citizens, except *maybe* "bad apples" like dirty bomb suspect Jose Padilla, and wasn't he a gang member anyway?); to state and federal agencies' dragging their feet on releasing documents legally available through open government laws; and to legislators such as Senator Mike DeWine (R-Ohio) constantly pushing the limits of the USA PATRIOT Act. (DeWine wants to allow the FBI to wiretap legal immigrants on the weakest "suspicion" of criminal activity.)

We've become trained to show up hours earlier to airports and to shuffle passively through security checkpoints, to unbuckle our pants and untuck our shirts, to hold our feet up in the air while agents wave wands over our shoes, to surrender nail clippers at the gate or just travel without them, to grin and bear it while Grandma's walker gets the once-over. (Who even remembers the relative ease of air travel pre-9/11—much less before the mid-'90s, when we first started showing picture IDs as a condition of flying?) We've already started to ignore the ubiquitous surveillance cameras like the ones that watched over us as we celebrated the Fourth of July on the Mall in Washington, D.C. We've learned to mock a never-ending series of proposals such as the infamous Operation Terrorist Information and Prevention System (TIPS) and plans for beefing up the old Neighborhood Watch program into a full-blown "national system for . . . reporting suspicious activity," both of which are moving forward in modified form despite widespread hooting.

Relinquishing civil rights does not make us safe

Has any of this made us safer? Not from our government, which has done little to earn our trust over the years, especially when it comes to law enforcement. And not from terrorists, either. If *they've* been cowed, it's because we went after bin Laden and his minions with specific, extreme, and righteous prejudice. It's because of regular people who took the terrorists down over Pennsylvania instead of the White House, and who wrestled shoe bomber Richard Reid onto the floor at 30,000 feet. It's because, as a nation and as individuals, we showed that we would fight for a way of life that values freedom and privacy.

How wrong, then, that we've dealt away some of our freedom and privacy for a promise of safety and security. To be sure, today's America is not [writer Jeremy] Bentham's *Panopticon* [which discusses a theme for improving prison discipline and establish an equitable legal system] or Orwell's dystopia [*1984*] (or even [Fidel] Castro's). It's not even solely a product of the September attacks, which merely hurried along trends that were already well under way. But in making the freedom-for-safety swap, we haven't just dishonored the dead of 9/11. We've helped something else die too.

6

Preemptive War Reduces Terrorism

Michael J. Glennon

Michael J. Glennon, professor of international law at the Fletcher School of Law and Diplomacy at Tufts University, is the author of many articles and books, including Limits of Law, Prerogatives of Power: Interventionism After Kosovo.

Anticipatory self-defense, or the doctrine of preemption, holds that it is acceptable for a state to attack a known hostile enemy before that enemy can attack it. Although prohibited by the United Nations Charter in 1945, anticipatory self-defense was necessary throughout the twentieth century, and it continues to be into the twenty-first. With the proliferation of weapons of mass destruction, to wait to be struck first could be devastating. Preemptive war is thus key to the security of the United States and is a legitimate option to reduce global terrorism.

The Bush Doctrine, as promulgated by President [George W.] Bush following the events of September 11 [2001, when terrorists flew planes into the World Trade Center and the Pentagon], contemplates preemptive use of force against terrorists as well as the states that harbor them. If the United Nations Charter is to be believed, however, carrying out that doctrine would be unlawful: The Charter permits use of force by states only in response to an armed attack. In 1945, when the Charter was framed, this prohibition against anticipatory self-defense may have seemed realistic. Today, it is not. Indeed, it is no longer binding law.

The UN and the right of survival

Since time immemorial, the use of force has been permitted in self-defense in the international as well as all domestic legal systems, and for much the same reason: With states as with individuals, the most elemental right is survival. So powerful has been its claim that the right of self-defense was considered implicit in earlier treaties limiting use of force by

Michael J. Glennon, "Preempting Terrorism: The Cause of Anticipatory Self-Defense," *The Weekly Standard*, January 28, 2002, pp. 24–27. Copyright © 2002 by News Corporation, Weekly Standard. All rights reserved. Reproduced by permission.

states; the Kellogg-Briand Peace Pact of 1928, like the 1919 Covenant of the League of Nations, made no mention of it.

In 1945, the right was made explicit. Article 51 of the United Nations Charter states expressly: "Nothing in the present Charter shall impair the inherent right of individual or collective self-defense if an armed attack occurs against a Member of the United Nations. . . ." Self-defense thus emerged as the sole purpose under the Charter for which states may use force without [UN] Security Council approval.

While the Charter professes not to "impair" the inherent right to self-defense, it does precisely that. Prior to 1945, states used defensive force *before* an attack had occurred, to *forestall* an attack. The plain language of Article 51 permits defensive use of force only *if* an armed attack occurs. If none has occurred, defensive force—"anticipatory self-defense"—is not permitted.

Why insist upon an actual armed attack as a precondition for the use of force?

This new impairment of the right of self-defense was widely seen as sensible when the Charter was adopted. States had often used the claim of self-defense as a pretext for aggression. (The Nazi defendants at Nuremberg [the post–World War II war criminal trials] argued that Germany had attacked the Soviet Union, Norway, and Denmark in self-defense, fearing that Germany was about to be attacked.) If profligate use of force was ever to be reined in, narrower limits had to be imposed. And those limits had to be set out with a bright line; qualifying defensive rights with words like "reasonable," "imminent," or even "necessary" would leave states too much discretion and too much room for abuse. The occurrence of an actual armed attack was thus set up as an essential predicate for the use of force. The new requirement narrowed significantly the circumstances in which force could be used. And it set out a readily identifiable and, it was thought, objectively verifiable event to trigger defensive rights. Phony defensive justifications would be less plausible and war would be less frequent, thereby vindicating the first great purpose of the Charter—"to maintain international peace and security."

The impairment was realistic, it was further thought, because the need for anticipatory defense would diminish. The reason was that the Security Council would pick up where individual states were now compelled by the Charter to leave off. The Council, to be equipped with its own standing or standby forces, was authorized to use force in response to any "threat to the peace"—authority far broader than that accorded individual states. Coupled with the requirement that states report to the Security Council when using defensive force, this new institution—this "constabulary power before which barbaric and atavistic forces will stand in awe," as [former British prime minister Winston] Churchill described it—would make anticipatory self-help a thing of the past.

All know that it didn't work out that way. Throughout the Cold War the Security Council deadlocked repeatedly on security issues. States never gave the Council the peace enforcement troops contemplated by the Charter's framers. The Council authorized (rather than used) force only haphazardly "to maintain or restore international peace and security." And, as discussed later, states continued to use force often, obviously not in response to armed attacks.

Forward-looking actions

Still, like most states, the United States never formally claimed a right to anticipatory self-defense—i.e., to use armed force absent an armed attack, so as to prevent one from occurring. During the 1962 Cuban Missile Crisis [when the USSR pointed missiles at the United States from Cuba] the United States declined to rely upon Article 51, claiming instead that the "quarantine" of Cuba was authorized by the Organization of American States (and implicitly by the Security Council). When Israel seemed to assert a right to use defensive force to prevent an imminent Arab attack in June 1967, and even when Israel squarely claimed that right in attacking an Iraqi nuclear reactor in 1981, the United States steered clear of the issue of anticipatory self-defense. In 1986, however, the United States finally did claim the right to use "preemptive" force against Libya following the bombing of a Berlin [Germany] night club that killed two Americans.

This last incident is worth considering closely: The Libyan bombing highlights the doctrinal confusion surrounding self-defense and also marks a proverbial "paradigm shift" in American thinking on the question. Why insist upon an actual armed attack as a precondition for the use of force? The axiomatic answer, under long-standing dogma, is of course that force is necessary to protect against the attack. But by acknowledging that its use of force against Libya was preemptive, the United States in effect moved beyond the conventional justification. The Berlin bombing was obviously over and finished; no use of force was, or conceivably could have been, instrumental in "defending" Americans killed at the Berlin club. The United States was not, in this sense, responding *defensively*. It was engaged in a forward-looking action, an action directed at future, not past, attacks on Americans. Its use of force against Libya was triggered by the Berlin attack only in the sense that that attack was *evidence of the threat of future attacks*. Evidence of Libyan capabilities and intentions sufficient to warrant preemptive force might well have taken (and, in fact, also did take) the form of intelligence reports. From a purely epistemological standpoint, no actual armed attack was necessary.

The problem lay in the future, not the past.

Although the United States did not spell out its thinking this explicitly, in later incidents it acted on precisely this future-looking rationale. True, the United States was in each instance able to argue that actual armed attacks had occurred. But in each of those subsequent incidents, the United States was *responding to evidence of future intent and capability*, not defending against past action. Its objective was to avert future attacks through preemption and deterrence.

In 1993, for example, the United States fired cruise missiles at the Iraqi intelligence headquarters in Baghdad following an alleged effort by Iraq to assassinate President [George H.W.] Bush. But the assassination attempt was long since over; the United States used force not to defend against illicit force already deployed, but to discourage such force from being deployed in the future. In 1998, the United States fired cruise missiles at a terrorist training camp in Afghanistan and a pharmaceutical plant in Sudan following attacks on U.S. embassies in Kenya and Tanzania. Again, the provocation had ended; in no way can the United States be seen as having defended itself against the specific armed attack to which its embassies had been subject.

So, too, with the use of force against Afghanistan following September 11.[1] The armed attack against the World Trade Center and the Pentagon was over, and no defensive action could have ameliorated its effects. The U.S. use of force was prompted by the threat of future attacks. And it was evidence of that threat—gleaned from multiple intelligence sources, not simply from the September 11 attack—to which the United States responded with its action against Afghanistan. That action could well have been warranted even if September 11 had never occurred. The problem lay in the future, not the past.

The United States had long ago accepted the logic of using armed force without waiting to be attacked.

In each of these incidents, the United States justified its action under Article 51 of the Charter, claiming to be engaged in the *defensive* use of force. But in fact something different was going on. In each incident, the United States was—as it acknowledged forthrightly following the 1986 bombing of Libya—engaged in the use of *preemptive* force. The two are not the same. The justification for genuine defensive force was set forth by U.S. Secretary of State Daniel Webster in the famous *Caroline* case of 1837. To use it, he wrote, a state must "show a necessity of self-defense, instant, overwhelming, leaving no choice of means, and no moment of deliberation." (This formula continues to be widely cited by states, tribunals, and commentators as part and parcel of the law of the Charter.) Obviously, in none of the incidents canvassed above can the American use of force be said to meet the *Caroline* standard. None of the American armed responses needed to be, or was, instant. In each the United States deliberated for weeks or months before responding, carefully choosing its means. Those means were directed not at *defending against* an attack that had already begun, but at *preempting*, or *deterring*, an attack that *could* begin at some point in the future.

In fact, the United States had long ago accepted the logic of using armed force without waiting to be attacked. In the early 1960s, President [John F.] Kennedy seriously considered launching a preemptive strike against the People's Republic of China to prevent it from developing nu-

---

1. American forces fought in Afghanistan in late 2001 to oust the Taliban government, which had given shelter to terrorist mastermind Osama bin Laden and his group al Qaeda, the perpetrators of the September 11, 2001, attacks.

clear weapons. In 1994, President [Bill] Clinton contemplated a preemptive attack against North Korea for the same reason. During the Cold War, the United States retained the option of launching its nuclear weapons upon warning that a nuclear attack was about to occur—before the United States actually had been attacked—so as to protect command and control systems that were vulnerable to a Soviet first strike.

Reasons to strike first

It thus came as no dramatic policy change when in the Bush Doctrine, the United States publicly formalized its rejection of the armed attack requirement and officially announced its acceptance of preemption as a legitimate rationale for the use of force. "Every nation now knows," President [George W.] Bush said on December 11, [2001], "that we cannot accept—and we will not accept—states that harbor, finance, train, or equip the agents of terror."

That formalization was overdue. Twenty-first-century security needs are different from those imagined in San Francisco in 1945.

First, as noted above, the intended safeguard against unlawful threats of force—a vigilant and muscular Security Council—never materialized. Self-help is the only realistic alternative.

Second, modern methods of intelligence collection, such as satellite imagery and communications intercepts, now make it unnecessary to sit out an actual armed attack to await convincing proof of a state's hostile intent.

Third, with the advent of weapons of mass destruction and their availability to international terrorists, the first blow can be devastating—far more devastating than the pinprick attacks on which the old rules were premised.

Self-help is the only realistic alternative.

Fourth, terrorist organizations "of global reach" were unknown when Article 51 was drafted. To flourish, they need to conduct training, raise money, and develop and stockpile weaponry—which in turn requires communications equipment, camps, technology, staffing, and offices. All this requires a sanctuary, which only states can provide—and which only states can take away.

Fifth, the danger of catalytic war erupting from the use of preemptive force has lessened with the end of the Cold War. It made sense to hew to Article 51 during the Cuban Missile Crisis, when two nuclear superpowers confronted each other toe-to-toe. It makes less sense today, when safe-haven states and terrorist organizations are not themselves possessed of preemptive capabilities.

Risks and costs

Still, it must be acknowledged that, at least in the short term, wider use of preemptive force could be destabilizing. The danger exists that some states threatened with preemptive action (consider India and Pakistan) will be all too ready to preempt probable preemptors. This is another variant of the quandary confronted when states, in taking steps to enhance their security, unintentionally threaten the security of adversaries thus find their own security diminished as adversaries take compensatory action.

Preemption is a legitimate option, and . . . preemption is lawful.

But the way out of the dilemma, here as elsewhere, is not underreaction and concession. The way out lies in the adoption of prudent defensive strategies calculated to meet reasonably foreseeable security threats that pose a common danger. Such strategies generate community support and cause adversaries to adapt perceptions and, ultimately, to recalibrate their intentions and capabilities. That process can take time, during which the risk of greater systemic instability must be weighed against the risk of worldwide terrorist attacks of increased frequency and magnitude.

The greater danger is not long-term instability but the possibility that use of preemptive force could prove incomplete or ineffective. It is not always possible to locate all maleficent weapons or facilities, thereby posing the risk that some will survive a preemptive strike and be used in retaliation. Similarly, if a rogue state such as Iraq considers itself the likely target of preemptive force, its leaders may have an incentive to defend with weapons of mass destruction—weapons they would not otherwise use—in the belief that they have nothing to lose. A reliable assessment of likely costs is an essential precondition to any preemptive action.

A legitimate option

These are the sorts of considerations that policymakers must weigh in deciding whether to use preemptive force. Preemption obviously is a complement, not a stand-alone alternative, to non-coercive policy options. When available, those options normally are preferable. The point here is simply that preemption is a legitimate option, and that—the language of the Charter notwithstanding—preemption is lawful. States can no longer be said to regard the Charter's rules concerning anticipatory self-defense—or concerning the use of force in general, for that matter—as binding. The question—the sole question, in the consent-based international legal system—is whether states have in fact agreed to be bound by the Charter's use-of-force rules. If states had truly intended to make those rules obligatory, they would have made the cost of violation greater than the perceived benefits.

They have not. The Charter's use-of-force rules have been widely and regularly disregarded. Since 1945, two-thirds of the members of the United Nations—126 states out of 189—have fought 291 interstate conflicts in which over 22 million people have been killed. In every one of those conflicts, at least one belligerent necessarily violated the Charter. In most of those conflicts, most of the belligerents claimed to act in self-defense. States' earlier intent, expressed in words, has been superseded by their later intent, expressed in deeds.

Rather, therefore, than split legal hairs about whether a given use of force is an armed reprisal, intervention, armed attack, aggression, forcible countermeasure, or something else in international law's over-schematized catalogue of misdeeds, American policymakers are well advised to attend directly to protecting the safety and well-being of the American people. For fifty years, despite repeated efforts, the international community has been unable to agree on when the use of force is lawful and when it is not. There will be plenty of time to resume that discussion when the war on terrorism is won. If the "barbaric and atavistic" forces succeed, however, there will be no point in any such discussion, for the law of the jungle will prevail. Completing that victory is the task at hand. And winning may require the use of preemptive force against terrorist forces as well as against the states that harbor them.

7

Preemptive War Does Not Reduce Terrorism

Charles W. Kegley Jr. and Gregory A. Raymond

Charles W. Kegley Jr. is a professor of international relations at the University of South Carolina. His publications include The Long Postwar Peace: Contending Explanations and Projections *and* International Terrorism: Characteristics, Causes, Controls. *Gregory A. Raymond teaches courses in international relations and comparative foreign policy at Boise State University.*

The adoption of preemption (attacking an enemy before it can attack) as U.S. policy poses a great threat to national and international security. While it does not make sense to stand idle while enemies amass to attack, one must distinguish intentions from capabilities. Just because a nation has the means to attack does not necessarily mean that it will. Adopting preemption as a national security doctrine is disastrous; history is rife with examples of preemptive war that backfired. Indeed, preemptive war does not reduce terrorism but instead ripens the conditions of war, poverty, and resentment that breed it.

In the immediate aftermath of the terrorist attacks on Sept. 11, 2001, the U.S. began a war against global terrorism. Soon thereafter, America abandoned its Cold War strategy of containment [a policy that confines a hostile actor or idea], embracing the doctrine of preemptive warfare aimed at attacking suspected aggressors before they could strike first. This, in turn, led to the invasion of Iraq in March, 2003.

The Bush doctrine of preemption

The Bush Administration's doctrine of preempting terrorists and rogue states, in what is called alternatively "forward deterrence" or "anticipatory self-defense," raises anew timeless moral and legal issues about the conditions under which, and purposes for which, a just war for self-defense is permissible to counter a threat to national security. What it has advanced as a new national security strategy is nothing less than an am-

Charles W. Kegley Jr. and Gregory A. Raymond, "Preemptive War: A Prelude to Global Peril?" *USA Today Magazine*, vol. 131, May 2003, p. 14. Copyright © 2003 by the Society for the Advancement of Education. Reproduced by permission.

putation of the normative pillar on which global society has been based at least since 1928, when the Kellogg-Briand pact outlawed war as an instrument of foreign policy. This radical revision of customary international law is leading the world into uncharted waters. If it becomes permissible to attack other international actors who do not pose an imminent threat, then, without a moral principle to guide international conduct, war is likely to increase.

Pres. [George W.] Bush first signaled the policy change he was initiating on June 1, 2002, at West Point. To his way of thinking, 9/11 created unprecedented "new deadly challenges" that necessitated new approaches and rules for statecraft. Chastising tyrants like Iraq's Saddam Hussein as international outlaws, the President announced that "We must be prepared to stop rogue states and their terrorist clients before they are able to threaten or use weapons of mass destruction against the United States and our allies and friends. . . . Traditional concepts of deterrence will not work against a terrorist enemy whose avowed tactics are wanton destruction and the targeting of innocents, whose so-called soldiers seek martyrdom in death. . . . The greater the threat, the greater the risk of inaction—and the more compelling the case for taking anticipatory action to defend ourselves, even if uncertainty remains as to the time and place of the enemy's attack. To forestall or prevent such hostile acts by our adversaries, the United States will, if necessary, act preemptively."

This reasoning soon thereafter became the cornerstone of The National Security Strategy of the United States of America (NSS), released on Sept. 17 [2002]. It reiterated Bush's West Point declaration that the era of deterrence [a strategy that avoids war] was over and preemption was an idea whose time had come. It then proceeded to assert that, "Given the goals of rogue states and terrorists, the United States can no longer solely rely on a reactive posture as we have in the past. . . . We cannot let our enemies strike first." The NSS added, "Nations need not suffer an attack before they can lawfully take action to defend themselves against forces that present an imminent danger of attack."

The extreme revisionism of the Bush doctrine undercuts a key preemptory norm in international law that underpins all others—the use of force cannot be justified merely on account of an adversary's capabilities, but solely in defense against its aggressive actions. Preemption represents a frontal rejection of Articles 2(4) and 51 of the United Nations Charter that condones war only in self-defense. It opens the door to military first strikes against adversaries, under the claim that their motives are evil and that they are building the military capabilities to inflict mass destruction.

Preemption is based on fear

It is not difficult to appreciate the grave dangers that have prompted this watershed in U.S. national strategy. The threats which provoked the President's extreme strategic response are real. Raison d'etat [being concerned with state survival at all costs] dictates that actions be taken for the preservation of the state, and, in these threatening circumstances, many find reasonable the claim that the national interest makes such countermeasures imperative. The temptation to attack first an adversary who might attack you is, of course, often overwhelming. Why stand by in the face of a potential threat? "An ounce of prevention is worth a pound of cure," a popular cliche advises. Better to hit an enemy before it attacks, than to be left prostrate. The thinking underlying the rationale is expressed well in [author] Umberto Eco's [book] *Baudolino*, where the protagonist argues, "Better to be rid at once of someone who does not yet threaten you, than leave him alive so that he may threaten you one day. Let us strike first."

That realpolitik [the advancement of the state above all else] logic was at the root of the NSS proposition that the "best defense is a good offense," and the premise behind the President's explanation in an Oct. 7, 2002, speech in Cincinnati that "We have every reason to assume the worst, and we have an urgent duty to prevent the worst from happening." A proactive policy through preemption is defined as necessary because it was argued that America "cannot wait for the final proof—the smoking gun—that could come in the form of a mushroom cloud."

If it becomes permissible to attack other international actors who do not pose an imminent threat, . . . war is likely to increase.

Fear is a great motivator. There are ample reasons to fear terrorists like Osama bin Laden and tyrants like Saddam. The threats are real in this age of globalization in which boundaries are no longer barriers to external threats, a suitcase nuclear bomb or a chemical/biological weapon can obliterate any American city, and a terrorist can strike anywhere and anytime. The U.S. is vulnerable, so there is an understandable compulsion to eliminate threats by any means available, including preemptive strikes.

Preemption is advocated as a policy, but what must be understood is that this strategy goes beyond that goal to a whole other level—to preventive war. The Bush doctrine transcends the established limitations of the use of armed force in self-defense against a prior armed attack. "The President is not 'reserving a right' to respond to imminent threats," wrote Duke University professor of international relations Michael Byers in the July 25, 2002, issue of *The London Review of Books*, "he is seeking an extension of the fight of self-defense to include action against potential future dangers."

As the wording of the Bush NSS illuminates, the line between preemption and prevention is blurry. How does one distinguish intentions from capabilities? Because an adversary amasses arsenals of weapons, does that necessarily mean that those weapons are for aggression instead of defense? Without knowledge of motives, prudence dictates worst-case assumptions. This invites the so-called "security dilemma" that results when one country's arms acquisitions provokes corresponding actions by alarmed adversaries, with the result that all participants in the arms race experience reduced security as their weaponry increases. Preemption addresses the danger by attacking first and asking questions about intentions later.

Preemption has had disasterous consequences

The quest to redefine international rules to permit preemptive strikes has deeper philosophical, ethical, and legal consequences for the long term, beyond its unforeseen immediate impact. Does it threaten to weaken international security and, paradoxically, U.S. national security as well? To probe this question, let us look briefly at some historical precedents to preemptive practices in order to put the current policy into perspective. Consider some salient illustrations that precede Bush's rationale:

• In the third Punic War fought between the Roman and Carthaginian empires (264–147 B.C.), after a 50-year hiatus, the Romans bought the advice of the 81-year-old [Roman politician] Cato the Elder. Consumed with the fear that renewed Punic [Carthaginian] power would culminate eventually in Roman defeat unless drastic military measures were taken, he ended every speech to the Roman Senate by proclaiming "Carthaginian esse delendum" (Carthage must be destroyed). Heeding Cato's advice, Rome launched a preventive war of annihilation and, in 146 B.C., some 500,000 Carthaginian citizens were destroyed in an act of mass genocide, and an entire civilization was obliterated. The foreign threat had been met; thereafter, no challenges to Roman hegemony existed—but at what cost? The Roman historian Polybius prophetically lamented, "I feel a terror and dread lest someone someday should give the same order about my own native city." Perhaps this led him to conclude that "it is not the object of war to annihilate those who have given provocation to it, but to cause them to mend their ways." Worse still, this preventive war can be said to have destroyed the soul of Rome. After it, Rome suffered a prolonged period of revolutionary strife, and much later found itself victim of the same savage preemptive measures by invaders it had once inflicted on Carthage. "Val victis" (Woe betide the defeated), the Romans cried after the city was sacked by the Gauls in 390 A.D. Is there an object lesson here? Read on.

• Dec. 7, 1941, was "a day that will live in infamy," as Pres. Franklin D. Roosevelt declared in reaction to Japan's sneak attack on Pearl Harbor. That strike removed most of the U.S. Pacific fleet and thereby redressed the Japanese-American military balance of power. The attack was premeditated, for arguably preventive purposes—to hit the U.S. before it could use its superior military capabilities to smother Japanese imperialism and Japan's Asian Co-Prosperity Sphere [Japan's allies and trading partners] in its cradle. However, preventive action hardly proved practical. It backfired, provoking the sleeping American giant from isolationistic neutrality into an angry wrath without restraint, leading to the annihilating atomic bombing of Hiroshima on Aug. 6, 1945.

• In June, 1981, Iraq was making rapid headway, with French assistance, toward building a nuclear reactor. Israeli warplanes destroyed that facility in a strike that prevented Iraq from acquiring nuclear weapons. The attack was planned, and, with pinpoint accuracy and effectiveness, the potential threat (that [Israeli] Prime Minister Menachem Begin regarded as the most-serious challenge to Israeli self-preservation) was removed. Begin, a former terrorist, undertook terrorism against a proven terrorist and tyrant, thus practicing the same strategy he sought to contain. As G. John Ikenberry, the Peter F. Krogh Professor of Geopolitics and Global Justice at Georgetown University, notes, this attack broke normative barriers, "and the world condemned it as an act of aggression"—as unjustifiable and shortsighted. The Reagan Administration condemned the strike; France pronounced it "unacceptable"; and Great Britain berated it as "a grave breach of international law." The strategy worked, however, in the short run, as Iraqi plans for cross-border attacks on Kuwait, Iran, and, in all likelihood, Israel were averted. In the long run, though, the preventive attack strengthened Saddam's grip on power at home and animated his military ambitions to try harder—in the name of defense.

History is thus replete with examples of states that have rationalized preemptive surgical attacks against a rival for preventive purposes. In fact, it is hard to find many cases of states that did not claim that, in initiating war, they were merely acting prudently in self-defense. Nearly all wars have been justified by that claim. This record suggests that preventive war is a problem, not a solution.

The rules will change for all

Bush asserts that, "If we wait for threats to fully materialize, we will have waited too long." That justification has been voiced by many before as an excuse for war. As *New York Times* columnist Bill Keller observes, historians cite as U.S. examples of preemptive interventions "Woodrow Wilson's occupation of Haiti in 1915, Lyndon Johnson's dispatch of U.S. Marines to the Dominican Republic in 1965, and Ronald Reagan's invasion of Grenada in 1983. [But] while preemption has been an occasional fact of life, [until George W. Bush] no president has so explicitly elevated the practice to a doctrine. Previous American leaders preferred to fabricate pretexts [such as] the sinking of the [USS] *Maine*[1] . . . rather than admit they were going in 'unprovoked.'"

If a permissive climate of opinion on the acceptability of preemptive and preventive warfare takes root, will the U.S. and the world at large be safer and more secure? The normative barriers to the first-strike initiation of war vanish in a world in which preemption for prevention is accepted. Let us examine the blaring downside of the U.S. advocacy of preemptive warfare.

Preemption addresses the danger by attacking first and asking questions about intentions later.

Preemption and its extension to preventive war is a direct challenge to prevailing norms. To encapsulate the international legal consensus prior to 9/11, before U.S. doctrine began to challenge it, one might say that international law over time had gravitated toward increasingly restrictive sets of rules for justified war making. Aggressive war was illegal, but defensive war was not. International law, therefore, did not break down whenever war broke out, for there are specified conditions under which states were permitted to wage a war. Those criteria were highly restrictive, though, confining war to serve as a penal method for punishing a prior attack by an aggressor.

How the U.S. chooses to act—its code of conduct—will be a powerful

---

1. The sinking of the USS *Maine* was an accident, but it was blamed on Spain and used as grounds to start the Spanish-American War in 1898.

determinant of the rules followed throughout the international arena. Global leaders lead in creating the system's rules. When the reigning hegemon abandons an established rule and endorses a substitute one, the rules change for everyone. What the strongest do eventually defines what everybody should do, and when a practice becomes common it tends to be seen as obligatory. As Harvard University professor of international relations Stanley Hoffmann puts it, rules of behavior become rules for behavior.

How the U.S. chooses to act—its code of conduct— will be a powerful determinant of the rules followed throughout the international arena.

Changing circumstances call for changes in policy, and extreme times of trouble invite extreme responses. However, policies engineered in crises have rarely proven wise. In judging the ethics of a proposed standard of action, it is enlightening to recall German philosopher Immanuel Kant's insight into the situation. In his famous principle, the "categorical imperative," Kant asked humanity to consider, when contemplating an action or a policy, what the consequences would be if everyone practiced that same conduct. In evaluating the probity and prudential value of an action, he counseled that the sole ethical international activity is one that would be advantageous for humanity if it were to become a universal law practiced by all. Would that activity make for a better world? If all behave accordingly, as the practice becomes customary, would humanity benefit or suffer?

Kant preached an ethic that springs from the question "What if everybody did that?" and applied it to international relations. He believed, that the best reason for abiding by the ethics of Jesus Christ as propounded in the Sermon on the Mount was that those nonviolent principles would make for a better, more rewarding life for all, and that killing creates a hell on Earth. We should treat others as we ourselves would wish to be treated, because those actions will, reciprocally, provoke others to treat us as we treat them. Nonaggression thus serves not only our best ideals, but benefits our self-interest, as reciprocity in altruism creates better relationships and a better world in which to live. This is the realism of idealism.

The U.S. has an obligation to put forth peace

Taking this a short step forward, other questions can be asked about the moral responsibilities of the strong and mighty. What are the obligations of the powerful? How should they react to threats from weaker states? In asymmetrical contests of will, where the playing field is strongly slanted to the advantage of a superpower such as the U.S., should it play according to the same rules as its enemies? Lowering itself to the modus operandi [operational methods] of the likes of Saddam can reduce the U.S. superpower to the standards of those it opposes. Flexing military muscles without an international mandate and without convincing justification can prostitute traditional and honorable American principles, erode the U.S.'s reputation, and undermine its capacity to lead. To practice what is not right is to sacrifice respect for a country's most valuable asset—its reputation for virtue, the most important factor in what is known as "soft power" in the exercise of global influence.

Can smashing perceived threats serve justice efficiently? Recall moral philosopher John Rawls' simple test of justice—"Would the best off accept the arrangements if they believed at any moment they might find themselves in the same place of the worst off?." Historian Christopher Dawson provided a partial answer when he noted that, "As soon as men decide that all means are permitted to fight an evil, then their good becomes indistinguishable from the evil they set out to destroy."

Applying this reasoning, what is likely to result if global norms are redefined to permit all states to defend themselves against potential threats in advance, before an enemy undertakes an attack or inflicts an injury? What if the U.S. doctrine becomes every state's and every terrorist movement's policy?

Nonaggression thus serves not only our best ideals, but benefits our self-interest, as reciprocity in altruism creates better relationships and a better world in which to live.

What the big powers do sets the standards that others follow. If other states act on the same rationale the U.S. has promulgated and take preventive military action against any enemy they claim is threatening them, the right to use force will be legitimized. The danger is that every country could conclude that preemption for preventive purposes is an acceptable practice. This doctrine of preemption would invite any state to attack any adversary that it perceived was threatening it.

Preemption endangers the U.S. and the world

Perhaps unwittingly, the Bush Administration appears not to have taken into consideration the probability that its doctrine will encourage most others to accept that same doctrine, or that a bottomless legal pit will be created. "The specific doctrine of preemptive action," argues [professor] Ikenberry, "poses a problem: once the United States feels it can take such a course of action, nothing will stop other countries from doing the same." Indeed, that prophecy has already been fulfilled as others have emulated the American position by taking "up preemption as a way of dealing with these problems. The Bush doctrine—or at best the rhetoric—has already been appropriated by Russia against Georgia, by India against Pakistan. The dominoes can be expected to fall if the strategy of preemption continues to spread, as surely it will if the United States pursues its new policy." Or, as [columnist] Keller opines, "If everyone embraces [the U.S.] new doctrine, a messy world would become a lot messier. Caveat pre-emptor."

If a permissive climate of opinion on the acceptability of preemptive and preventive warfare takes root, will the U.S. and the world at large be safer and more secure? That is doubtful. It has taken a long time for an international consensus to build behind the view that a preemptive attack to prevent an enemy's potential attack is outside the boundaries of justified warfare. In earlier epochs, states believed that they could attack another country for any reason deemed in the attacker's national interests. That climate of normative opinion has evaporated, and, partially as a consequence, the frequency of interstate war has steadily declined and almost vanished since the Cold War ended. Now, however, the U.S. has justified preemptive war under the claim that the benefits of preemption exceed the costs of acting only on retaliation for prior attacks for defense.

This shift is not a cure; it is a curse. In pleading for preservation of the restrictive norms that prohibit preemptive strikes, historian Paul Schraeder, writing in *The American Conservative*, warns that the universal values "are changeable, fragile, gained only by great effort and through bitter lessons of history, and are easily destroyed, set aside, or changed for the worse for the sake of monetary gain or individual interest. And the fate of these norms and standards depends above all on what great powers, especially hegemons and superpowers do with them and to them. . . . The American example and standard for preemptive war, if carried out, would invite imitation and emulation, and get it. . . . A more dangerous, illegitimate norm and example can hardly be imagined. As could easily be shown by history, it completely subverts previous standards for judging the legitimacy of resorts to war, justifying any number of wars hitherto considered unjust and aggressive. [And] one can easily imagine plausible scenarios in which India could justly attack Pakistan or vice versa, or Israel or any one of its neighbors, or China Taiwan, or South Korea North Korea, under this rule that suspicion of what a hostile regime might do justifies launching preventive wars to overthrow it."

The Bush Administration has been vocal about the urgent need it perceives to do something about the dangers that confront U.S. security, but silent about the consequences that are likely to follow from that doctrinal shift to preemptive warfare. Do we really want to remove the normative handcuffs on the use of force? Do we really want to return to the free-wheeling unrestricted sovereign right of any and all rulers to define for themselves when they are threatened, so as to license anticipatory preemptive warfare? Europe experimented with that Machiavellian basis for international statecraft in the 17th century during the deadly Thirty Years' War, which reduced its population by a third. Autonomy makes for global anarchy. Is severing normative anchors on permissible warfare that demonstrably have reduced its incidence really an idea that serves American and global interests and ideals? This radical departure in radical times looks increasingly like a path to peril and a road to ruin.

8

Military Might Is the Best Way to Reduce Terrorism

Alan W. Dowd

Alan W. Dowd has written numerous articles on U.S. foreign policy, terrorism, national security, the military, and a wide variety of other topics. He is a frequent contributor to the World & I, National Review Online, American Outlook, *the* Washington Times, American Outlook Today, *and* American Legion Magazine.

The war on terrorism can only be won by expanding military operations to every corner of the globe. Indeed, every international conflict should be viewed as an extension of the war on terrorism. If foreign governments cannot or will not reign in terrorists originating from their nations, the United States must either send troops to help them do it or topple uncooperative regimes. In order to pursue such a wide-reaching campaign, military spending must once again become America's top priority. The war on terrorism must quickly become a truly global military campaign lest the terrorist network become too large to be defeated.

Long before he served in the Bush administration, Defense Secretary Donald Rumsfeld began collecting little morsels of common and not-so-common sense. Dubbed "Rumsfeld's Rules," the collection of wit and wisdom is virtually required reading in Washington. However, with the next step in the War on Terror hindered by . . . worries over a wider war, it appears that at least one of Rumsfeld's rules is being ignored: "If a problem cannot be solved, enlarge it."

The war on terror must span the globe

The problem, of course, is terrorism and its patrons, architects and infrastructure. That means the problem extends far beyond Afghanistan [where terrorists hide]. If nothing else, September 11 [2001, when terrorists attacked America] taught the United States that terrorism's war on civilization cannot be contained to faraway places, within tidy geo-

51

graphic boundaries. Consequently, neither can civilization's war on terrorism. As Rumsfeld observed during the early phases of the war in Afghanistan, "The only way to deal with these terrorist threats is to go at them where they exist . . . to take the battle to where they are."

However, doing that over the long haul requires the American people, along with their government and military, to reevaluate the way they look at the entire world, as they did at the outset of the Cold War. This simply has not yet occurred in the War on Terror. Until it does—until the war becomes an overlay for every hotspot and conflict on the globe, a prism through which everything else is considered—the roots of global terrorism will remain intact. And America's anti-terror campaign will not achieve what the American people demand.

The first step in reversing this course is to follow Rumsfeld's rules, and enlarge the problem. In short, mission creep [that is, the expansion of a military operation] should not only be expected in the War on Terror—it should be encouraged.

Different enemies, same problem

But how large is large enough? President George W. Bush was on the right track last September [2001], when he spelled out the doctrine that bears his name. "Our enemy," he explained, "is a radical network of terrorists and every government that supports them." The network extends into 60 countries, many of which oppose terrorism but lack the means to combat it. This category includes such disparate places as Indonesia, Malaysia, the Philippines, Somalia, Georgia and even Colombia.

Next, there are countries that, in Bush's words, "oppose terror, but tolerate the hatred that leads to terror." Sudan and Saudi Arabia fall into this category. Until last October, so did Pakistan. However, in the intervening months, Pakistan has proven with words and actions that it is indeed an ally in the War on Terror. The picture is not so clear for the Saudis and Sudanese.

"If a problem cannot be solved, enlarge it."

Finally, there is the hard core of terrorism. We know them well, some of them too well—Libya, [Palestinian leader Yasir] Arafat's Palestine, Syria, Iran, Iraq and North Korea. Of course, even this group can be broken down into subgroups. Libya is slowly limping away from its old ways. Given the right incentives or pressures, Syria and proto-Palestine might choose the path of reform. Iran has a growing reform movement of its own, while the regimes in Iraq and North Korea seem sadly beyond reform or repair.

Still, the United States cannot wage the War on Terror based on hope and hypotheticals. Washington must deal with the hard facts of the here and now. The facts are that along with terrorist organizations such as al Queda, the al-Aqsa Martyrs and others, these governments have come together at what Bush calls "the perilous crossroads of radicalism and technology." Some have money, some have intelligence capabilities, some have technology, some have personnel, some have weapons of mass destruction, and all of them have motive. Whether they comprise an "axis of evil" [Bush's term for Iraq, Iran, and North Korea] or something else is irrelevant. These groups and states do exist, and as long as they continue to poison the planet, they are a threat to the civilized world.

As America learned on September 11, it is better to pay in treasure than with blood.

Unraveling terror's hard core will obviously be far more difficult than toppling the heroin dealers who ruled Afghanistan. As former British Prime Minister Margaret Thatcher observes, they "have had years to entrench themselves, and they will not be dislodged without fierce and bloody resistance." However, Thatcher's words should not dissuade America from carrying this war into the very heart of the global terror network. To borrow the parlance of the Cold War, the United States must be prepared to roll back every regime that supports terror. This is not to say that US troops need to be omnipresent for the war to be successful. However, it does mean that if a government is unable to move against terrorists inside its borders, the US military will have to help (as it has in Georgia and the Philippines). And if a government refuses that help, it is choosing war—the kind of war visited upon the Taliban [the former rulers of Afghanistan], the kind of war it will not survive.

The United States must not stray from its course

In the immediate aftermath of September 11, the Bush administration seemed to be guided by this grim reality. Then came Israel's springtime counteroffensive in Ramallah,[1] followed by nuclear saber-rattling in Kashmir,[2] and the nascent War on Terror bogged down. Rather than incorporating these conflicts into the wider war, the White House seemed determined to quarantine its anti-terror campaign from them. As the spiral of events in South Asia and across the Middle East illustrates, this is a self-defeating proposition. Each terrorist attack, indeed each day these terror states and sub-state groups survive, advances their common cause and undermines civilization's.

As evidence, just consider the past year, which saw terror's footsoldiers strike symbols of modernity in New York and Karachi [Pakistan], institutions of stability in Delhi [India] and Washington, expressions of religious pluralism in Islamabad [Pakistan] and Netanya [Israel]. In just 12 months, the enemy killed 3547 people, wounded another 1080, destabilized global economic markets, threatened friendly governments from Israel to India to Indonesia, exposed deep fissures between the United States and its friends in Europe, sent the Asian subcontinent careening to-

---

1. In spring 2002, Israel attacked Palestinian leader Yasir Arafat's compound in the city of Ramallah to retaliate for suicide bombings that had been carried out in Israel.   2. Kashmir is a disputed territory between Pakistan and India. Tensions over Kashmir have brought the two nuclear powers to the brink of war several times.

ward a nuclear holocaust, and helped derail Washington's plans to carry the war beyond Afghanistan.

When viewed through the prism of the War on Terror, these events—most of which occurred *after* the US-led liberation of Afghanistan—spell victory for the terrorists. And such disparate events will continue to translate into small victories for the enemies of civilization and small defeats for the civilized world until Washington recognizes these conflicts for what they are—local fronts in a global war.

Now is no time for timidity. Once it is unfettered, the US military can be the most fearsome force on earth.

Thankfully, there are indications that the White House is doing just that. After a season of hedging, the summer of 2002 became a turning point of sorts for the Bush administration. "We must take the battle to the enemy, disrupt his plans and confront the worst threats before they emerge," the president declared during a June visit to West Point. Three weeks later, he put some of those enemies on notice: "I call on the Palestinian people to elect new leaders, leaders not compromised by terror," he intoned. "Every nation actually committed to peace must block the shipment of Iranian supplies to . . . regimes that promote terror, like Iraq," he added. "And Syria must choose the right side in the war on terror by closing terrorist camps and expelling terrorist organizations."

Military spending is of utmost importance

The United States has good reason to put these regimes in its crosshairs: Once armed with nuclear or chemical weapons, these government and their terror partners could destroy not buses in Tel Aviv or buildings in Manhattan, but entire cities.

To prevent that, Bush has unveiled a "preemptive strike" doctrine, which promises to be costly. But as America learned on September 11, it is better to pay in treasure than with blood. As in 1941, 1951 and 1981, defense spending must again become a national priority. In its first post–September 11 budget, the White House earmarked $369 billion for defense—a 12 percent increase over the previous year. The OMB [Office of Management and Budget] estimates defense outlays of $4.5 trillion over the next decade. However, given the kind of war that lies ahead, even this figure may be too low. As Rumsfeld observed in testimony before the Senate in February [2002], "In the Eisenhower and Kennedy era, we were spending about 10 percent of our gross national product on defense [and] over 50 percent of the federal budget on defense." The 2003 defense budget, by comparison, amounts to just 17 percent of the overall federal budget and a scant 3.3 percent of GDP. According to historian Mark Helprin, if the United States invested merely "the peacetime average of the last half-century," its current defense budget would be $655 billion. If the American people refuse to muster even that with 3000 of their countrymen erased without warning or cause, they never will.

Of course, the American people haven't really been asked to make such a sacrifice. But history reminds us that they will, as long as the president makes a persuasive case. [President Franklin Delano Roosevelt] had to convince an isolationist America to aid Great Britain prior to America's entry into World War II. [President] Harry Truman had to make the case for [organizing the North Atlantic Treaty Organization, or] NATO and the Marshall Plan [which helped rebuild Europe after World War II]. On top of postwar reconstruction, [President] Dwight Eisenhower asked the American people to double defense spending, fueling a costly and brutal arms race with Moscow—an arms race [President] Ronald Reagan ended with a withering volley of military spending in the 1980s that ballooned the national debt.

Still, solving a problem this large will require more than new military doctrines and new arsenals. It will require a genuine transformation of the United States government. Washington's decision to create a Department of Homeland Security may signal that such a transformation is underway. Among other things, the new department is forcing the nation to rethink security and brace for what President John Kennedy might have called a long, twilight struggle against terror. Bringing together such disparate agencies as the INS [Immigration and Naturalization Service], Coast Guard, Customs Service, FEMA [Federal Emergency Management Agency], and the Nuclear Incident Response office, the reorganization is both a substantive public-policy initiative and a symbolic example of the political-governmental transformation the nation must undergo to win this war.

Finally, if the War on Terror matures into a truly global campaign, US military commanders will have to become as audacious and fearless as the men they are sending into battle. But this all-important transformation of the military-command mindset is progressing slowly. . . .

Americans have grown increasingly impatient and squeamish over these decades. In the shadow of Vietnam, the American people demanded short, painless wars. And the Pentagon delivered, each mini-war conditioning the American public to expect less blood and less sacrifice than the previous conflict. And this, in turn, conditioned the US military to be overly cautious, curbing its audacity and leading inevitably to more low-risk, low-impact wars. . . .

[But] now is no time for timidity.

The military is America's best weapon

Once it is unfettered, the US military can be the most fearsome force on earth. Japan learned that in April 1942, just four months after the sneak attack on Pearl Harbor. Doing the unthinkable, Lt. Col. Jimmy Doolittle used Navy aircraft carriers to launch Army bombers into the skies over Tokyo. The bombers arrived in broad daylight, throwing a stunning counter-punch at Japan's once-invulnerable homeland and foreshadowing the war's devastating final blow.

When [Soviet leader Joseph] Stalin tried to squeeze the allies out of Berlin by blockading the city's western half, Lt. Gen. Curtis LeMay blended the principles of strategic bombing with the efficiency of a Detroit assembly line to sustain a city for an entire year and win the first battle of the Cold War. When all seemed lost in Korea, it was Gen. Douglas

MacArthur who did the impossible by landing at Inchon, crushing the North Koreans and rescuing South Korea.

A dozen years later, when the [Soviet Union] tried to tip the nuclear balance in Cuba [during the Cuban Missile Crisis], the [United States] used a mix of restraint and rapid reflexes to face down Moscow and stave off Armageddon. As he watched the United States gather its forces and form a fist during those thirteen days in October, an awe-struck General de Gaulle is reported to have remarked, "There is really only one superpower."

What was true in 1962 remains true today. After all, that's one reason why America was attacked on September 11, and it's why only the United States can marshal the resources needed to solve this problem. But if America fails to enlarge the problem and transform itself, terrorism's war on civilization may soon grow too large and too deadly to be solved at all.

9

Intelligence Gathering Is the Best Way to Reduce Terrorism

Joel Garreau

Joel Garreau is a staff writer for the Washington Post. *He has also authored* Edge City: Life on the New Frontier *and* The Nine Nations of North America.

Terrorist organizations are human networks, not armies. They rely on trust, relationships, and communication to operate. Military operations and bombing campaigns will be ineffective against such groups because they will not destroy the trust and connections those networks are built upon. Therefore, the most effective way to reduce terrorism is to wage a war of wits. With good intelligence gathering techniques, authorities can learn who the key terrorists are and either eliminate them or tarnish their reputations in the eyes of others in the network. Unraveling the ties that bind terrorists will win the war on terrorism.

The essence of this first war of the 21st century is that it's not like the old ones. That's why, as $40 billion is voted for the new war on terrorism, 35,000 reservists are called up and two aircraft carrier battle groups hover near Afghanistan,[1] some warriors and analysts have questions:

In the Information Age, they ask, how do you attack, degrade or destroy a small, shadowy, globally distributed, stateless network of intensely loyal partisans with few fixed assets or addresses?

If bombers are not the right hammer for this nail, what is?

Bombers worked well in wars in which one Industrial Age military threw steel at another. World War II, for instance, was a matchup of roughly symmetrical forces.

This is not true today.

1. American forces fought in Afghanistan in late 2001 to oust the Taliban government, which had given shelter to terrorist mastermind Osama bin Laden and his group al Qaeda.

Joel Garreau, "A Battle of Wits," *The Washington Post National Weekly Edition*, September 24–30, 2001. Copyright © 2001 by the Washington Post Book World Service/Washington Post Writers Group. Reproduced by permission.

That's why people who think about these things call this new conflict "asymmetric warfare." The terrorist side is different: different organization, different methods of attack—and of defense.

"It takes a tank to fight a tank. It takes a network to fight a network," says John Arquilla, senior consultant to the international security group Rand and co-author of the forthcoming "Networks and Netwars: The Future of Terror, Crime and Militancy."

He asks: "How do you attack a trust structure—which is what a network is? You're not going to do this with Tomahawk missiles or strategic bombardment."

"It's a whole new playing field. You're not attacking a nation, but a network," says Karen Stephenson, who studies everything from corporations to the U.S. Navy as if they were tribes. Trained as a chemist and anthropologist, she now teaches at Harvard and the University of London. "You have to understand what holds those networks in place, what makes them strong and where the leverage points are. They're not random connections," she says.

Human networks are distinct from electronic ones. They are not the Internet. They are political and emotional connections among people who must trust each other in order to function, like Colombian drug cartels and [Spanish] Basque separatists and the Irish Republican Army. Not to mention high-seas pirates, smugglers of illegal immigrants, and rogue brokers of weapons of mass destruction.

But how to [destroy] a network?

The good news is that in the last decade we have developed a whole new set of weapons to figure that out.

Analyze networks to destroy key links

An industry has arisen to help corporations build new networks and junk old hierarchical bureaucracies in the age of merging and emerging companies, says Kathleen Carley, director of the Center for Computational Analysis of Social and Organizational Systems at Carnegie Mellon University. New tools have been developed that analyze how an organization interacts, yielding a kind of X-ray that shows where the key links are.

There is a general set of principles to any network, says Stephenson, whose company, NetForm, has developed software that mathematically analyzes networks.

She points out that typically a network is made up of different kinds of nodes—pivotal people.

> *"It takes a tank to fight a tank. It takes a network to fight a network."*

The critical ones are "hubs," "gatekeepers" and "pulsetakers," she believes. Hubs are the people who are directly connected to the most people; they know where the best resources are and they act as clearinghouses of information and ideas, although they often are not aware of their own importance. Gatekeepers are those connected to the "right" people. They are the powers around the throne, and often they know their own importance. Pulsetakers are indirectly connected to a lot of people who know the right people. They are "friends of a friend" to vast numbers of people across widely divergent groups and interests.

The classic example of how to use this analysis is "finding the critical employee in the company—the lone expert who knows how to fix the machine," Carley says. Ironically, without network analysis, managers frequently don't recognize who that is and the nature of his importance.

"You know those little cameras that some people have on top of their monitors? Let me just say that it is entirely possible to . . . look through them without the machine being turned on."

"But there's no reason it can't be turned around in the opposite way," she says. There's no reason organizational glitches, screw-ups, jealousies and distrust that slow and degrade performance can't be intentionally introduced [in order to damage a network]." A network's ability to adapt to new challenges can be degraded.

Carley says: "One of the things that leads to the ability to adapt is who knows who and who knows what. The higher that is, the better the group's flexibility. But you can reduce the number of times the group can communicate or congregate. Or you can rotate personnel rapidly." And in war, this may have to be done by capturing or killing them. "You can also segregate the things people are doing, so they learn only on a need-to-know basis. The more isolated the tasks are, the more you inhibit their ability to function as a team.

"Imagine in your office if you knew who went to whom for advice," Carley says. "If you found a set of people who gave out more advice than anyone else and then removed them from the network, so they can't communicate with others, you would infringe on the ability of the network to operate."

Targeting terrorism using the network approach

In the case of terror networks, people are linked by family ties, marriage ties and shared principles, interests and goals. They thus can be all of one mind, even though they are dispersed and devoted to different tasks. They "know what they have to do" without needing a single-central leadership, command or headquarters.

There is no precise heart or head that can be targeted, Arquilla says. Even if you take out an Osama bin Laden [that is, a terrorist] his organization, al Qaeda ("The Base"), still has the resilience of a classic human network. Bin Laden's, for instance, is made up of an estimated two dozen separate militant Islamic groups in the Philippines, Lebanon, Egypt, Kashmir, Algeria, Indonesia and elsewhere, with hundreds of cells, some of them located in Western Europe and even the United States, as we've now discovered.

On the other hand, depending on the structure of the network, removing a few key nodes can sometimes do a lot of good, says Frank Fukuyama, author of the seminal work "Trust: The Social Virtues and the Creation of Prosperity" and now a professor at the School of Advanced International Studies at Johns Hopkins University.

"Some are so tightly bound to each other that they are not embedded in other networks. Kill a few nodes, and the whole thing collapses. Take the case of the [terrorist group] *Sendero Luminoso* [Shining Path] in Peru. It couldn't have been that hierarchical. It was designed for the mountains of Peru. It couldn't have been terribly centralized. It had a scattered cell structure. It was hard to infiltrate. It was dispersed. And yet when you got [Shining Path founder and leader Abimael] Guzman and a few top aides, the entire thing fell apart.

"The idea that there is no end of terorrists, no way to stamp them all out, that if you kill a hundred, another hundred will spring up—I would be very careful of that assumption. The network of people who are willing to blow themselves up has to be limited. Sure, there are sympathizers and bagmen and drivers. But the actual core network of suicide bombers is probably a much smaller population. It is also tight-knit and hard to infiltrate. But it is limited. It is not obvious to me that there is an endless supply."

Corrupting the network

Another tactic: advancing the cause of the weakest link.

"Suppose I've got a really powerful pulsetaker," says Stephenson, "vying for a position of dominance. But I also know that a member of the blood kin group is moving forward who is weaker. If you arrange an accident to eliminate the pulsetaker, and let the weaker family member come in, you've helped corrupt the network."

The beauty of seeding weakness into an organization is that you can degrade its effectiveness while still monitoring it, and not causing a new and potentially more efficient organization to replace it. "You don't want to blow away the organization. You want to keep some fraudulent activity going on so you can monitor it. If you blow them away, you lose your leads," says Stephenson. "Better the devil you know. Like [Libyan dictator] [Moammar] Gaddafi. Keep him alive, because you know him. Who knows what sort of clever mastermind might replace him."

Intelligence is crucial to analyze the network's weak links so you can destroy it.

In a war between human networks, the side with superior intelligence wins.

"You're talking about what amounts to a clan or a tribe or brotherhood of blood and spilled blood. That is really tough to crack. Trying to infiltrate it—we're talking years," says David Ronfeldt, a senior social scientist at Rand. However, from outside the network you can also look for patterns that stand out from the norm, like who talks to whom, e-mail exchanges, telephone records, bank records and who uses whose credit cards, says Ronfeldt.

"I would attack on the basis of their trust in the command and control structures by which they operate," says Arquilla. "If they believe they are being listened to, they will be inhibited. If we were to reduce their trust in their infrastructure, it would drive them to non-technical means—force them to keep their heads down more. A courier carrying a disk has a hell of a long way to go to communicate worldwide. If you slow them down, interception is more likely."

Technology and spying

Human networks are distinct from electronic networks. But technology is the sea in which they swim.

"What made [networks] vulnerable historically is their inability to coordinate their purpose," says Manuel Castells, author of "The Rise of the Network Society," the first volume of his trilogy, "The Information Age."

"But at this point," he says, "they have this ability to be both decentralized and highly focused. That's what's new. And that's technology. Not just electronic. It's their ability to travel everywhere. Their ability to be informed everywhere. Their ability to receive money from everywhere."

This is why Arquilla is dubious about some traditional intelligence-gathering techniques, and enthusiastic about new ones. For instance: You can talk about turning one of the network members over to your side, but "that's problematic," he says. "You don't know if they're playing you as a double agent or are simply psychotic." He is also dubious about the value of satellite reconnaissance in determining what we need to know about these networks.

Find a member of the enemy group who is clearly a harmless idiot; treat him as if he were the most important figure and the only one worthy of being taken seriously.

However, Arquilla likes the idea of understanding how the network works by using clandestine technical collection [using technology to spy]. For instance, he says, when any computer user surfs on the Web—looking for travel tickets, say—more often than not a piece of software, called a cookie, is transmitted to his computer. The device monitors his every move and reports back to some database what he's done.

Now, Arquilla says, "think of something much more powerful than cookies." They exist, he says. One way to use them is by creating "honey pots." This involves identifying Web sites used by activists or setting up a Web site that will attract them, and seeding [the honey pots] with these intelligent software agents. When the activists check in, they can't leave without taking with them a piece of software that allows you to backtrack, getting into at least one part of the enemy network. "That likely gives you his/her all-channel connections, and maybe even some hints about hubs or the direction of some links," says Arquilla.

There are other possibilities.

"You know those little cameras that some people have on top of their monitors? Let me just say that it is entirely possible to activate those and operate them and look through them without the machine being turned on," he says.

Software also exists that "allows you to reconstruct every single keystroke. One after the other. Why is that important? If you do find the right machine, you can reconstruct everything that [was typed]. Even with unbreakable encryption, you have all the keystrokes."

Unless we have a fundamental rethinking of strategic matters, . . . [the war on terror] will be desperate missile attacks at the wrong targets with a lot of suffering.

Much of this is hardly new, of course, divide and conquer has worked for a long time. Whenever the police got a Mafia wiseguy—Joe Valachi, for instance—to betray the others, no Mafiosi could trust another one as much anymore. Machiavelli, in "The Prince" of 1505, wrote about the strategic deployment of betrayal to undermine trust.

What's different is our technological ability to track groups in real time and see patterns that may be invisible on the surface. "Our technology is sufficient that you can now handle realisticized groups. We can deal with 30 to several thousand," says Carley. "You couldn't do that before."

Ways to outsmart the terrorist network

In 1996, Arquilla and Ronfeldt wrote a slim but highly prescient volume called "The Advent of Netwar" for the National Defense Research Institute, a federally funded research and development center sponsored by the Office of the Secretary of Defense, the Joint Chiefs of Staff and the defense agencies.

It predicts that in a war between human networks, the side with superior intelligence wins. It also makes some tactical suggestions about countering human networks with counter-networks that actually have been used to combat computer hackers.

They include:

- Find a member of the enemy group who is clearly a harmless idiot; treat him as if he were the most important figure and the only one worthy of being taken seriously.
- Single out competent and genuinely dangerous figures; write them off or call their loyalty to the cause into question.
- Control the stories people tell each other to define their reason for living and acting as they do. The terrorist story, says Ronfeldt, "gives these people common cause—us versus them. Right now the U.S. would seem to have the edge at the worldwide level. But within the region, there was the dancing in the streets in Palestine. Part of the story is that America's evil, and that America's presence is to blame for so many of the problems in the Middle East. We have to attack that part."

- Find the list of demands extorted by the network; grant some that make no sense and/or disturb and divide their political aims.
- Paint the enemy with PR ugly paint [public relations slander] so that they seem beyond the pale, ridiculous, alien, maniacal, inexplicable.
- Destroy their social support networks by using "helpful" but differently valued groups that are not perceived as aggressive.
- Divide and conquer; identify parts of the network that can be pacified and play them against former allies.
- Intensify the human counter-networks in one's own civil society.

Adds Manuel Castells: "We should be organizing our own networks, posing as Islamic terrorist networks. We should then demand to join one of these networks and then destroy the trust structures. Only way to infiltrate. Oldest technique in the world."

Few of these ideas involve flattening Kabul [Afghanistan], all of these analysts note.

Stephenson worries that massing the Navy near Afghanistan is "a symbolic show of old-fashioned strength. It's not about that anymore. This whole playing ground has shifted."

"In order to do anything, you cannot be blind," says Castells. "The most extraordinary vulnerability of the American military is it looks like they do not have many informants inside Afghanistan. It also looks like the majority of the components of this network do not relate directly or essentially to nation-states. That is new. Unless we have a fundamental rethinking of strategic matters, it's going to be literally, literally exhausting and impossible. It will be desperate missile attacks at the wrong targets with a lot of suffering.

10

Racial Profiling
Reduces Terrorism

Richard Lowry

In addition to being a regular contributor to the National Review, *Richard Lowry is the author of* Legacy: Paying the Price for the Clinton Years.

Political correctness threatens to make obsolete one of America's most valuable terrorist-fighting tools: racial profiling. Because it is primarily Islamic Arabs who commit terrorist acts against the United States, they should be scrutinized over other ethnic groups. Such ethnic profiling is not a matter of discrimination; it is simply common-sense security. Current profiling systems that do not take into account race, ethnicity, or national origin undermine efforts to prevent attacks. Indeed, checking everyone, or checking people arbitrarily in the interest of appearing fair wastes time and fails to concentrate energy on who is most likely to be dangerous. Applying racial profiling to screening systems is the most common-sense way to reduce terrorism in America.

In late September [2001], M. Ahsan Baig was kept off United Flight 288 from San Francisco to Philadelphia because the pilot didn't like the way he seemed to be furtively talking to another passenger in the waiting area. Baig, a California computer specialist who is from Pakistan, got on another flight 90 minutes later after apologies from a ticket agent. An hour-and-a-half delay, for many fliers, might be considered a good day at the airport. For Baig, it was the occasion for a civil-rights lawsuit.

So it goes at the nation's airports. An Arab-American Secret Service agent's recent difficulty boarding a flight with his gun has become a national scandal. Meanwhile, discrimination lawsuits filed by Arab-American men have become the latest cause of aspiring Erin Brockoviches.[1] [The terrorist attacks of] September 11 [2001] may have changed the world, but grievance politics is one corner of it that has been serenely untouched. Arab-American groups still scream at any suggestion of com-

1. that is, people who expose unethical practices and contest their legality

monsense security at airports, while the Bush administration still cowers at any association with "racial profiling." It has become clear . . . that the pieties of American racial politics will remain unchanged—even after contributing to a mass murder.

Racial profiling would have prevented September 11

No one likes to say it out loud, but more than half the people on the FBI's Most Wanted terrorist list are named Mohammed, Ahmed, or both (for instance, Ahmed Mohammed Hamed Ali). Islamic terrorists will necessarily be Muslims, and probably from the Arab world. Not to profile for those characteristics is simply to ignore the nature of today's terrorism. As security expert Neil Livingstone points out, when the Black Panthers[2] were hijacking planes in the 1970s, security personnel should have been on the lookout for young black men; when D.B. Cooper—the famed skyjacker who parachuted out of a plane with a bagful of cash in 1971—was on the public mind, security should have been suspicious of young-to-middle-aged white men booked to fly over rugged terrain.

Profiling of a sort has been an official practice of the nation's airlines for years. In 1994, Northwest [Airlines] began to develop a computer-assisted passenger pre-screening system (CAPPS) to single out high-threat passengers. After the TWA Flight 800 disaster in July 1996,[3] the Clinton administration convened a [former vice president] Al Gore–led commission to study aviation security. This commission recommended that the Northwest system be adopted by the airline industry generally. But, under pressure from Arab-American and civil-liberties groups, it insisted that profiling not rely "on material of a constitutionally suspect nature—e.g., race, religion, or national origin of U.S. citizens." The profiles instead would use factors such as whether someone had bought a one-way ticket or paid cash for it. . . .

Islamic terrorists will necessarily be Muslims, and probably from the Arab world. Not to profile for those characteristics is simply to ignore the nature of today's terrorism.

CAPPS, then, had served its political function [by being politically correct and appeasing people]. Its security function was another matter. Not all terrorists are idiots, so they might attempt to avoid the behavior that triggers the profiling system. For example, they can buy round-trip tickets and use credit—thus easily slipping by two of the CAPPS criteria. According to the *Wall Street Journal*, CAPPS managed to flag two of the September 11 hijackers, Nawaf Alhazmi and Khalid Al-Midhar, who commandeered Flight 77, the Pentagon plane. They had reserved their tickets by

2. The Black Panthers were a militant black power group active during the 1960s and 1970s. They advocated violence as a way of attaining equal rights for blacks in the United States. 3. On July 17, 1996, TWA Flight 800 crashed into the Atlantic Ocean off the coast of New York. While the National Transportation Safety Board officially labeled the disaster as an accident, theories abound that the jet was the target of a terrorist attack.

credit card, but paid in cash. While their checked bags were supposedly more carefully checked, neither of them was searched or questioned at the airport—lest, presumably, they complain to the Council on American-Islamic Relations.

And so, they went on their way. If ethnicity and national origin were among the CAPPS criteria, all of the September 11 hijackers probably would have been flagged. And, as the Manhattan Institute's Heather Mac Donald has pointed out, if personal searches and questioning had been routine, a bizarre pattern might have become clear—why so many Arabs in first class? why so many box cutters?—and the whole plot come undone. Other countries have had exactly this experience. In a famous 1986 case, a pregnant woman booked on an El Al flight from Heathrow [airport in London, England] to Tel Aviv [Israel] was pulled aside (pregnant women don't usually travel alone). After questioning, it was discovered that, unbeknownst to her, her Jordanian boyfriend had planted a bomb in her carry-on bag that would have killed all 375 people on her flight. It is inarguable that sensitivity about profiling in the U.S. made the September 11 hijackers' job easier.

Their plot would have simply been a non-starter in Israel. There, passengers are divided into three categories: Israelis and foreign Jews, non-Jewish foreigners, and anyone with an Arab name. Those in the third category get lots of special attention, including being taken to a special room for baggage and body checks. Arab passengers can be interrogated up to three different times. The philosophy is to concentrate resources on the more likely threats, and not waste them on low-risk passengers. As one former Israeli security official told the Associated Press, if everyone got the most vigorous treatment, the planes would never get off the ground.

But the Israeli system requires a tough-mindedness that is in short supply in the U.S. On the issue of profiling, transportation secretary Norman Mineta's ignorance appears to be nearly invincible. Mineta's Japanese-American family was interned during World War II.[4] He implies at every opportunity that by standing in the way of ethnic profiling, he is preventing a similar enormity today. "A very basic foundation to all of our work," he says, "is to make sure that racial profiling is not part of it." Asked on *60 Minutes* if a 70-year-old white woman from Vero Beach [Florida] should receive the same level of scrutiny as a Muslim from Jersey City [New Jersey], Mineta said, "Basically, I would hope so."

Ethnic profiling is not discrimination

Mineta pulls no rhetorical punches: "Surrendering to actions of hate and discrimination makes us no different than the despicable terrorists who rained such hatred on our people." Since Mineta thinks "discrimination" includes ethnic profiling, this must be one of the laziest statements of post–September 11 moral equivalence. . . . The airlines are only too happy

---

4. During World War II, the U.S. government rounded up people of Japanese descent, citizens and noncitizens, and placed them in internment camps for the duration of the war. In later years, the internment of the Japanese was widely criticized for being discriminatory, unjust, and paranoid. The experience has been cited as a reason why profiling and other types of ethnic targeting should not be pursued in the name of security.

to play along. A September 21 [2001] memo to Delta employees from CEO Fred Reid has the subject line "Tolerance," and disavows ethnic profiling in the strongest possible terms: "We cannot afford to follow this tragic behavior. It is exactly what our enemies are striving for: the end of our open, diverse, and tolerant way of life."

If you believe the feds, the airlines have a legal obligation to ape the federal line. In memos sent to the airlines after September 11, the Transportation Department has constantly claimed that the law forbids profiling on the basis of ethnicity or national origin: "Various federal statutes prohibit air carriers from subjecting a person in air transportation to discrimination on the basis of race, color, national origin, religion, sex, or ancestry." I called a spokesman at Transportation to confirm that the department meant to suggest that ethnic profiling constituted illegal discrimination. He was adamant that this was so.

It is inarguable that sensitivity about profiling in the U.S. made the September 11 hijackers' job easier.

But this is, at best, a misreading of the law. Discrimination in public conveyances has been outlawed for a long time, but that was meant to forbid things like forcing blacks to ride on the back of the bus. The circumstances of airline security are, of course, entirely different. Profiling at airports would not be classic New Jersey Turnpike "racial profiling," where police mark out a whole class of people as more likely than average to be transporting drugs, and then stop large numbers of them. Airport profiling would respond to a specific threat to commit a specific crime (more suicide hijackings) made by a specific group (the Islamic terrorists of [the terrorist network] al-Qaeda). It would be less analogous to New Jersey, then, than to a recent case in Oneonta, N.Y. The courts endorsed the right of police there to stop and examine almost every black man in that small town after an elderly woman said she had been attacked by a black assailant whose hand was cut in their scuffle.

Our current system is absurd

So, the airlines and the federal government are not legally required but instead are freely choosing to collaborate in a system that no one considers secure, while creating the maximum inconvenience and delays. It's a system that features the false egalitarianism [that is, fake equality] of the anti-profilers. One of the recommendations of the Gore commission's in-house anti-profiling panel was that "the procedures applied to those who fit the profile should also be applied on a random basis to some percentage of passengers who do not fit the profile." This idea has been adopted on a massive scale, which accounts for much of the absurdity of flying today: ditzy celebrities, children, and older women subjected to the same excruciating security as a 25-year-old man just arrived from Riyadh [Saudi Arabia].

There are many problems with this. The first is one of justice. It burdens people whom we have absolutely no reason to believe have any chance of being terrorists, just to create an appearance at airports that will make young male Arabs feel better. The second is that the time and resources spent getting the proverbial Vero Beach 70-year-old to take off her white sneakers could be better spent searching and questioning a passenger who has a higher chance of being a terrorist. Finally, there is the matter of economics.

If the pilot hadn't noticed that the angry guy trying to board his plane with a gun looked like all of the September 11 terrorists, he would have been a fool.

Long lines make people marginally less likely to fly, which pushes airlines that much closer to bankruptcy. The only way to reduce lines in the current system would be to add more security checkpoints. But that's not easy. It means hiring more screeners, when it is difficult to have enough competent ones to fill the current slots; it means spending more money, when airlines are already bleeding; and it bumps up against a physical constraint at many airports, which may not have more room for screening checkpoints. The same problem applies to examining checked luggage—there is so much of it and so few machines that doing all of it well and quickly will be impractical for years.

Racial profiling can work

It obviously makes sense to find ways to whittle down the security load. The answer is to separate out passengers according to the threat they represent, probably into three groups. One would be members of an enhanced frequent-flyer program, with travelers voluntarily undergoing a background check and getting a fool-proof biometric ID card in return for fewer security hassles. (The airport in Amsterdam [Netherlands] already has such a program, which includes an eye scan.) Arab-American travelers could opt into such a program, and never again worry about being profiled. Then, there would be the unwashed masses, who would get more routine security treatment. The last category would be passengers profiled as potential risks, who could get a version of the full-bore Israeli scrutiny.

This would make everyone involved very uncomfortable, especially, of course, the targeted passengers. Almost all of them would be clean [that is, harmless]. The extra burden on young male Arab-Americans and Arab immigrants—the extra pat-down, the searching questions—would be very unfair in a cosmic sense, but an acceptable social cost given the stakes involved in preventing further attacks.

The fact that no one is systemically profiled on the basis of ethnicity and national origin now contributes to the nervousness of pilots, passengers, and security personnel who don't trust the current system and attempt to do amateur profiling on their own. A sophisticated computerized system would reduce the need for individual judgments after a passenger has already passed security checkpoints. But a pilot should still have the right to refuse a passenger, a privilege that goes back to old maritime law. It was this prerogative that was in play in the American Airlines/Secret Service agent case, as the pilot balked at carrying an agitated armed man whose paperwork wasn't properly filled out.

American, to its credit, has stood by the pilot, all the while insisting that the airline would never ethnically profile. But if the pilot hadn't noticed that the angry guy trying to board his plane with a gun looked like all of the September 11 terrorists, he would have been a fool. The Left [that is, liberals] talks often of "diversity," but is unwilling to acknowledge that the world's variousness might mean that certain ethnic groups are more likely to be terrorists than others. Willfully ignoring this fact contributed to September 11. Continuing to do so would heap criminal folly on top of willful recklessness. In a famous 1949 case, Justice Robert Jackson said that the Constitution is not "a suicide pact." Indeed, it isn't, but maybe our racial politics is.

11

Racial Profiling Does Not Reduce Terrorism

David Harris

David Harris is a professor of law at the University of Toledo College of Law and the author of Profiles in Injustice: Why Racial Profiling Cannot Work. *Harris is considered a leading authority on the issue of racial profiling; he has testified twice in the U.S. Senate and before many state legislative bodies on the issue.*

Just when the American public was about to relegate the practice of racial profiling—using a person's appearance as a factor in deciding who merits police attention—to the annals of failed policies, the attacks of September 11, 2001, brought the issue to the forefront. Although it may seem tempting to use racial profiling to apprehend future terrorists, a closer look at the practice makes it clear that doing so would in fact hinder America's ability to effectively reduce terror. In the past, engaging in racial profiling has not made law enforcement any more successful in reducing crime. Indeed, a helpful indicator of intent to harm is not how people look but how they behave; focusing on looks distracts authorities from identifying suspicious behavior. Most importantly, homing in on only one type of person ignores the fact that terrorists are of a multitude of ethnicities and nationalities.

In the aftermath of the September 11 [2001] tragedies in New York and Washington, DC, we Americans have heard countless times that our country has "changed forever." In many ways, especially in terms of national and personal security, this is quite true. Americans have always assumed that terrorism and other violent manifestations of the world's problems did not and would never happen here, that our geographic isolation by the Atlantic and Pacific Oceans protected us. Indeed, since the Civil War, the United States has experienced no sustained violence or war on its own soil. Sadly, we know now that we are vulnerable, and that like countries all over the world, we must take steps to protect ourselves. . . .

David Harris, "Flying While Arab: Lessons from the Racial Profiling Controversy," *Civil Rights Journal*, vol. 6, Winter 2002.

Racial profiling resurfaces

One of these [steps] has been particularly noticeable—both because it represents a radical shift in what we did prior to September 11, and because it also continues a public discussion that was taking place in our country before that terrible day. Racial profiling—the use of race or ethnic appearance as a factor in deciding who merits police attention as a suspicious person—has undergone a sudden and almost complete rehabilitation. Prior to September 11, many Americans had recognized racial profiling for what it is—a form of institutional discrimination that had gone unquestioned for too long. Thirteen states had passed anti-profiling bills of one type or another, and hundreds of police departments around the country had begun to collect data on all traffic stops, in order to facilitate better, unbiased practices. On the federal level, Congressman John Conyers, Jr., of Michigan and Senator Russell Feingold of Wisconsin had introduced the End Racial Profiling Act of 2001, a bill aimed at directly confronting and reducing racially biased traffic stops through a comprehensive, management-based, carrot-and-stick approach.

Using Arab or Muslim background or appearance to profile for potential terrorists will almost certainly fail.

September 11 dramatically recast the issue of racial profiling. Suddenly, racial profiling was not a discredited law enforcement tactic that alienated and injured citizens while it did little to combat crime and drugs; instead, it became a vital tool to assure national security, especially in airports. The public discussion regarding the targets of profiling changed too—from African Americans, Latinos, and other minorities suspected of domestic crime, especially drug crime, to Arab Americans, Muslims, and others of Middle Eastern origin, who looked like the suicidal hijackers of September 11. In some respects, this was not hard to understand. The September 11 attacks had caused catastrophic damage and loss of life among innocent civilians; people were shocked, stunned, and afraid. And they knew that all of the hijackers were Arab or Middle Eastern men carrying out the deadly threats of Osama bin Laden's al Qaeda terrorist network based in the Middle East, which of course claims Islam as its justification for the attacks and many others around the world. Therefore, many said that it just makes sense to profile people who looked Arab, Muslim, or Middle Eastern. After all, "they" were the ones who'd carried out the attacks and continued to threaten us; ignoring these facts amounted to some kind of political correctness run amok in a time of great danger.

But if the renewed respectability and use of profiling was one of the ways in which September 11 changed things, we might also notice that the "new" racial profiling demonstrated the truth of an old saw: the more things change, the more they stay the same. We should remember that racial profiling of African Americans and Latinos also originated in a war—the metaphorical "war on drugs"—and was justified with the same arguments. But even more importantly, we should learn from what we now know were the grand mistakes of profiling in the last 10 years. If we do that, we will see that using Arab or Muslim background or appearance to profile for potential terrorists will almost certainly fail—even as it damages our enforcement efforts and our capacity to collect intelligence.

A history of fear

As in almost any serious policy inquiry, a look at the history of our country can help us attain a proper perspective on how to view what we do now. Unfortunately, that history gives us reasons to feel concern at this critical juncture. Any serious appraisal of American history during some of the key periods of the 20th century would counsel an abundance of caution; when we have faced other national security crises, we have sometimes overreacted—or at the very least acted more out of emotion than was wise.

In the wake of World War I, the infamous Palmer Raids resulted in the rounding up of a considerable number of immigrants. These people were deported, often without so much as a scintilla of evidence. During World War II, tens of thousands of Japanese—immigrants and native born, citizens and legal residents—were interned in camps, their property confiscated and sold off at fire-sale prices. To its everlasting shame, the U.S. Supreme Court gave the internment of the Japanese its constitutional blessing in the infamous Korematsu case. It took the United States government decades, but eventually it apologized and paid reparations to the Japanese. And during the 1950s, the Red Scare resulted in the mining of lives and careers and the jailing of citizens, because they had had the temerity to exercise their constitutionally protected rights to free association by becoming members of the Communist Party years or even decades before.

> *When police agencies used race or ethnic appearance as a factor . . . they did not get the higher returns on their enforcement efforts that they were expecting.*

Hopefully, we can see the common thread that runs through these now notorious examples: an apprehension of danger to the country not only from the outside but from a group of people within who are identified racially, ethnically, or politically with those thought to pose the threat, and a willingness to take measures that sweep widely through the identified group—more widely than the threat might justify. (Of course, we have also learned that these threats have been wildly exaggerated; for example, the discovery of government documents more than four decades after the internment of the Japanese showed that the government misled the courts by intentionally withholding critical information that contradicted official efforts to make the case for a sufficiently severe threat to justify the internment.) The threat we face now bears many similarities: a danger from overseas posed by one group, and an identified group in the United States that has come under suspicion. All of this ought to encourage us not to leap forward with racial or ethnic profiling, but to hesitate before we do.

We must hope that we have learned the lessons of this history—that the emotions of the moment, when we feel threatened, can cause us to damage our civil liberties and our fellow citizens, particularly our immigrant populations. And it is this legacy that should make us think now, even as we engage in a long and detailed investigation of the September 11 terror attacks. As we listen to accounts of that investigation, reports indicate that the investigation has been strongly focused on Arab Americans and Muslims. What's more, private citizens have made Middle Eastern appearance an important criterion in deciding how to react to those who look different around them. Many of these reports have involved treatment of persons of Middle Eastern descent in airports.

Race and ethnic appearance are very poor predictors of behavior.

In itself, this is not really surprising. We face a situation in which there has been a terrorist attack by a small group of suicidal hijackers, and as far as we know, all of those involved were Arabs and Muslims and had Arabic surnames. Some or all had entered the country recently. Given the incredibly high stakes, some Americans have reacted to Middle Easterners as a group, based on their appearance. In a way, this is understandable. We seldom have much information on any of the strangers around us, so we tend to think in broad categories like race and gender. When human beings experience fear, it is a natural reaction to make judgments concerning our safety based on these broad categories, and to avoid those who arouse fear in us. This may translate easily into a type of racial and ethnic profiling, in which—as has been reported—passengers on airliners refuse to fly with other passengers who have a Middle Eastern appearance.

Racial profiling has not reduced crime

The far more worrying development, however, is the possibility that profiling of Arabs and Muslims will become standard procedure in law enforcement. Again, it is not hard to understand the impulse; we want to catch and stop these suicidal hijackers, every one of whom fits the description of Arab or Muslim. So we stop, question, and search more of these people because we believe it's a way to play the odds. If all the September 11 terrorists were Middle Easterners, then we get the biggest bang for the enforcement buck by questioning, searching, and screening as many Middle Easterners as possible. This should, we think, give us the best chance of finding those who helped the terrorists or those bent on creating further havoc.

But we need to be conscious of some of the things that we have learned over the last few years in the ongoing racial profiling controversy. Using race or ethnic appearance as part of a description of particular suspects may indeed help an investigation; using race or ethnic appearance as a broad predictor of who is involved in crime or terrorism will likely hurt our investigative efforts. All the evidence indicates that profiling Arab Americans or Muslims would be an ineffective waste of law enforcement resources that would damage our intelligence efforts while it compromises basic civil liberties. If we want to do everything we can to secure our country, we have to be smart about the steps we take.

As we think about the possible profiling of Arabs and Muslims, recall the arguments made for years about domestic efforts against drugs and crime. African Americans and Latinos are disproportionately involved in drug crime, proponents of profiling said; therefore concentrate on them. Many state and local police agencies, led by the federal Drug Enforcement Administration, did exactly that from the late 1980s on. We now know that police departments in many jurisdictions used racial profiling, especially in efforts to get drugs and guns off the highways and out of the cities. For example, state police in Maryland used a profile on Interstate 95 during the 1990s in an effort to apprehend drug couriers. According to data from the state police themselves, while only 17 percent of the drivers on the highway were African American, over 70 percent of those stopped and searched were black. Statistics from New Jersey, New York, and other jurisdictions showed similar patterns: the only factor that predicted who police stopped and searched was race or ethnicity. No other factor—not driving behavior, not the crime rate of an area or neighborhood, and not reported crimes that involved persons of particular racial or ethnic groups—explained the outcomes that showed great racial or ethnic disproportionalities among those stopped and searched.

As any experienced police officer knows, what's important in understanding who's up to no good is not what people look like, but what they do.

But as we look back, what really stands out is how ineffective this profile-based law enforcement was. If proponents of profiling were right—that police should concentrate on minorities because criminals were disproportionately minorities—focusing on "those people" should yield better returns on the investment of law enforcement resources in crime fighting than traditional policing does. In other words, using profiles that include racial and ethnic appearance should succeed more often than enforcement based on other, less sophisticated techniques. In any event, it should not succeed less often than traditional policing. But in fact, in departments that focused on African Americans, Latinos, and other minorities, the "hit rates"—the rates of searches that succeeded in finding contraband like drugs or guns—were actually lower for minorities than were the hit rates for whites, who of course were not apprehended by using a racial or ethnic profile. That's right: when police agencies used race or ethnic appearance as a factor—not as the only factor but one factor among many—they did not get the higher returns on their enforcement efforts that they were expecting. Instead, they did not do as well; their use of traditional police methods against whites did a better job than racial profiling, and did not sweep a high number of innocent people into law enforcement's net.

The reason that this happened is subtle but important: race and ethnic appearance are very poor predictors of behavior. Race and ethnicity describe people well, and there is absolutely nothing wrong with using skin color or other features to describe known suspects. But since only a very small percentage of African Americans and Latinos participate in the drug trade, race and ethnic appearance do a bad job identifying the particular African Americans and Latinos in whom police should be interested. Racial and ethnic profiling caused police to spread their enforcement activities far too widely and indiscriminately. The results of this misguided effort have been disastrous for law enforcement. This treatment has alienated African Americans, Latinos, and other minorities from the police—a critical strategic loss in the fight against crime, since police can only win this fight if they have the full cooperation and support of those they serve. And it is precisely this lesson we ought to think about now, as the cry goes up to use profiling and intensive searches against people who look Arab, Middle Eastern, or Muslim.

Profiling will not catch terrorists

Using race, ethnic appearance, or religion as a way to decide who to regard as a potential terrorist will almost surely produce the same kinds of results: no effect on terrorist activity; many innocent people treated like suspects; damage to our enforcement and prevention efforts.

Even if the suicide hijackers of September 11 shared a particular ethnic appearance or background, subjecting all Middle Easterners to intrusive questioning, stops, or searches will have a perverse and unexpected effect: it will spread our enforcement and detection efforts over a huge pool of people who police would not otherwise think worthy of attention. The vast majority of people who look like Mohammed Atta and the other hijackers will never have anything to do with any kind of ethnic or religious extremism. Yet a profile that includes race, ethnicity, or religion may well include them, drawing them into the universe of people who law enforcement will stop, question, and search. Almost all of them will be people who would not otherwise have attracted police attention, because no other aspect of their behavior would have drawn scrutiny. Profiling will thus drain enforcement efforts and resources away from more worthy investigative efforts and tactics that focus on the close observation of behavior—like the buying of expensive one-way tickets with cash just a short time before takeoff, as some of the World Trade Center hijackers did.

The unhappy truth is that we just don't know what the next group of terrorists might look like.

This has several important implications. First, just as happened with African Americans and Latinos in the war on drugs, profiling of Arabs and Muslims will be overinclusive—it will put many more under police suspicion of terrorist activity than would otherwise be warranted. Almost all of these people will be hard-working, tax-paying, law-abiding individuals.

While they might understand one such stop to be a mere inconvenience that they must put up with for the sake of national security, repetition of these experiences for large numbers of people within the same ethnic groups will lead to resentment, alienation, and anger at the authorities.

Second, and perhaps more important, focusing on race and ethnicity keeps police attention on a set of surface details that tells us very little and draws officers' attention away from what is much more important and concrete: behavior. The two most important tools law enforcement agents have in preventing crime and catching criminals are observation of behavior and intelligence. As any experienced police officer knows, what's important in understanding who's up to no good is not what people look like, but what they do. Investigating people who "look suspicious" will often lead officers down the wrong path; the key to success is to observe behavior. Anyone who simply looks different may seem strange or suspicious to the untrained eye; the veteran law enforcement officer knows that suspicious behavior is what really should attract attention and investigation. Thus focusing on those who "look suspicious" will necessarily take police attention away from those who act suspicious. Even in the current climate, in which we want to do everything possible to prevent another attack and to apprehend those who destroyed the World Trade Center and damaged the Pentagon, law enforcement resources are not infinite. We Americans must make decisions on how we run our criminal investigation and prevention efforts that move us away from doing just anything, and toward doing what is most effective.

It seems extremely unlikely that they will use people for their next attack who look like exactly what we are looking for.

Third, if observation of suspicious behavior is one of law enforcement's two important tools, using profiles of Arabs, Muslims, and other Middle Easterners can damage our capacity to make use of the other tool: the gathering, analysis, and use of intelligence. There is nothing exotic about intelligence; it simply means information that can be useful in crime fighting. If we are concerned about terrorists of Middle Eastern origin, among the most fertile places from which to gather intelligence will be the Arab American and Muslim communities. If we adopt a security policy that stigmatizes every member of these groups in airports and other public places with intrusive stops, questioning, and searches, we will alienate them from the enforcement efforts at precisely the time we need them most. And the larger the population we subject to this treatment, the greater the total amount of damage we inflict on law-abiding persons.

And of course the profiling of Arabs and Muslims assumes that we need to worry about only one type of terrorist. We must not forget that, prior to the attacks on September 11, the most deadly terrorist attack on American soil was carried out not by Middle Easterners with Arabic names and accents, but by two very average American white men: Timothy McVeigh, a U.S. Army veteran from upstate New York, and Terry Nichols, a farmer from Michigan [who were involved with the bombing of the Al-fred P. Murrah Building in Oklahoma City in 1995]. Yet we were smart enough in the wake of McVeigh and Nichols' crime not to call for a profile emphasizing the fact that the perpetrators were white males. The unhappy truth is that we just don't know what the next group of terrorists might look like. . . .

We cannot discount the obvious skill and determination of the adversaries we face in this struggle. The September 11 attacks made clear that the al Qaeda terrorists were not wild, unguided fanatics. Rather they showed a high degree of intelligence and cunning, spotting and taking advantage of unnoticed weaknesses in our immigration and aviation security systems. They showed the ability and the patience for long-range planning and careful action, as well as strict self-discipline. All of this is, of course, in addition to a belief in their own cause so strong that they were willing to sacrifice their own lives to attain their goals. And we cannot forget that the attack on the World Trade Center on September 11 was not the first, but the second attempt to destroy those buildings; their first attempt, in 1993, was unsuccessful, and they watched, waited, and planned for eight years to try again. With enemies of such craftiness and determination, it seems extremely unlikely that they will use people for their next attack who look like exactly what we are looking for. Rather, they will shift to light-skinned people who look less like Arabs or Middle Easterners, without Arabic names, or to people who are not Middle Easterners at all, such as individuals from African nations or the Philippines. (In both places, there are significant numbers of Muslims, a small but significant number of whom have been radicalized.) This, of course, will put us back where we started, and racial or ethnic appearance will become a longest-of-long-shot, almost certainly an ineffective predictor at best, and a damaging distracting factor at worst.

The terrorist attacks in New York and Washington, DC, present us with many difficult choices that will test us. We will have to ask ourselves deep questions: Who are we, as a nation? What is important to us? What values lay at the core of our Constitution and our democracy? How will we find effective ways to secure ourselves without giving up what is best about our country? The proper balance between safety and civil rights will sometimes be difficult to see. But we should not simply repeat the mistakes of the past as we take on this new challenge. Only our adversaries would gain from that.

12

Immigration Must Be Restricted to Reduce Terrorism

Richard D. Lamm

Richard D. Lamm is the former governor of Colorado.

One of the most pressing but neglected subjects in the war on ter-rorism is the relationship between immigration and terrorism. For example, the terrorists responsible for the September 11, 2001, at-tacks entered the country from the Middle East legally, although many of their visas had expired before the attacks. Tightening the border and restricting immigration are as critical to reducing ter-rorism as are military operations abroad. The United States must improve its ability to do background checks on people seeking visas to enter the country. It must also employ more immigration officers and apply moratoriums to visa applicants from countries known to sponsor terrorism. In addition, the United States must curb illegal immigration so as to get a better handle on exactly who is in the country. Finally, a tamper-proof national identifica-tion card must be issued to cut down on illegal immigration and prevent identity theft.

Editor's Note: The following speech was delivered at a seminar at Daniels Col-lege of Business in Denver, Colorado, on January 17, 2002.

September 11, 2001 [when terrorists flew planes into the World Trade Center and the Pentagon] is the date on which the nature of warfare changed. It is not enough to say—as many do—that "everything changed" or that "the world will never be the same." We owe our country and each other to be specific and comprehensive. We need to assess what we learned and speculate and debate what we have yet to learn. The lessons we do not learn from September 11th will come back to haunt us.

Terrorism and immigration

I would suggest the most important factor that changed on September 11th was the type of warfare that we must protect ourselves against. One of the most important but most neglected subjects of the new national agenda is the relationship between immigration and terrorism. The 19 Islamic fundamentalists who wrought the destruction of September 11th and killed over 3,000 innocent people were all foreigners who had been in the United States from a week to three years. They apparently all entered the U.S. legally, though some of their visas had expired before September 11, 2001. No official of the U.S. knew where they were, what they were doing, nor did any alarm bells go off when they overstayed their visas. This was not unique, as approximately one-half of the 8 to 11 million illegal aliens in the U.S. entered with valid visas but overstayed their legal duration.

[Senator] Gary Hart and his National Commission on Terrorism warned of this immigration/terrorism relationship over a year ago. The National Commission on Terrorism concluded in a 2000 report that, "In spite of elaborate immigration laws and the efforts of the Immigration and Naturalization Service, the United States is, de facto, a country of open borders."

We must understand that the border is a critical tool for protecting America and we have to recognize and admit to ourselves how vulnerable we are. According to an article in the *Atlantic Monthly* we have 86 football stadiums that seat more than 60,000 people and 10 motor speedways with capacity over 100,000 spectators. The Indianapolis Speedway seats more than 250,000. We have 50 of the 100 tallest buildings in the world and the Mall of America gets 600,000 visitors a week. What good is the best airport security if our borders are open and we present targets like this?

We must understand that the border is a critical tool for protecting America and we have to recognize and admit to ourselves how vulnerable we are.

The actions of September 11th were acts of war carried out against our civilian population by foreign civilians who came here legally and who lived, played, worked, and went to school in the United States. There is every reason to suspect that a number of additional terrorists are here in the U.S. right now. Many more have vowed to come here and commit their own acts of terror. Thousands of Islamic schools in various parts of the world are teaching millions of impressionable children to "hate America" and that we are "The Great Satan". A chorus of voices warns us that there will be additional acts of terrorism on American soil and that these terrorists are either hiding in plain sight or seeking lawful admission. We ignore the immigration lessons of September 11th at our great peril.

We face a ruthless, fanatical foe that flies civilian airplanes into buildings and is dedicated to killing Americans. In other wars the nation had to deal with domestic security, but as an extension of some foreign war. The new reality is that America is now the battlefield and every American is a potential target. The problem is larger than "foreigners" of course. Let us not forget that Timothy McVeigh was an American and the FBI's best guess is that the anthrax attacks were most likely domestic terrorism.

The state of the border

The border is an important tool in preventing terrorism. As every house has to have a door, every country has to have a border. We have been singing, "We are the World" more than we have been singing "America The Beautiful." It is now imperative that we better monitor who we admit into this country, and insure that people honor the terms of their admission. We must monitor whom we admit where they are, whether they are going to the schools they were admitted to attend, and we must know when they leave or don't leave. The INS [Immigration and Naturalization Service] admits that there are 300,000 foreigners who have been ordered out of the country but have disappeared before they could be deported. THREE HUNDRED THOUSAND: that's as many people as live in Ft. Collins [Colorado].

We ignore the immigration lessons of September 11th at our great peril.

Interpol and our own intelligence people have found that the twentieth terrorist was not able to enter the U.S. from Germany because the U.S. refused him a visa. The border worked; the score—1 out of 20 terrorists coming here to do us harm. We should be thankful for that one, but this is not a good score. But because of that one visa denial, we can reasonably speculate that the plane that crashed in Pennsylvania missed its Washington, D.C. target because it only had 4 terrorists (instead of 5) and that [passenger] Todd Beamer and his "let's roll" brave band were able to frustrate the fourth plane's unidentified target in Washington, D.C.—albeit at the cost of their own lives.

Immigration reform will not solve the problem of terrorism, but this problem will not be solved without immigration reform. We talk a lot about non-immigration solutions to terrorism that are not realistic. According to the same *Atlantic Monthly* article, we would need 14,000 Air Marshals to cover every domestic flight, which is more than the total number of special agents in the FBI. We can run but we can't hide from the fact that we have an immigration/terrorist problem. We cannot fully protect America once people enter this country. It is now clear that all hijackers had documents and came in at an U.S. port of entry. Their names were checked against a "Watch list" and apparently no alarms went off.

We must do better. We must better evaluate the potential for harm that comes with visitors, students and immigrants. I suggest this visa part of the problem has at least two parts: (1) that many students and visitors received their visas in a country where it was impossible for American officials to do an adequate background check (2) that the U.S. counselor offices worldwide are understaffed and cannot adequately do background checks even if the sending country cooperates.

America had about 500 million border crossings [in 2001], 350 million of them non-U.S. citizens. Over seven million visas were issued to foreigners last year and another 2.4 million applicants for visas were denied. Most of the 31 million foreigners who enter the U.S. temporarily each year do so without visas under reciprocal visa waiver policies that permit nationals of 29 countries to enter the U.S. for up to 90 days without visas. One of the hijackers was a recently naturalized French citizen who entered under this waiver program. No visas are required for Mexicans and Canadians entering the US. with Border Crossing Cards that permit limited travel in the U.S.

Background checks and illegal immigration

First I suggest we pass into federal law a suggestion of [California] Senator Dianne Feinstein who submitted a bill for a six-month moratorium on visas from countries who sponsor terrorists. In 1998 America issued 564,683 student visas including over 7,999 from Saudi Arabia, 4,500 from Pakistan, 2,000 from Jordan, and 1,600 from Egypt. I think it is a reasonable question whether we are or even can do adequate background checks from these terrorist sponsoring countries. While a moratorium on visas pending a review of the procedure for the issuance of visas seems only common sense to most of us, America's universities, including my own, vehemently protested this legislation and it died. It should be resurrected. How could we possibly take the risk of giving a student or tourist visa to someone from Iran, Iraq, Syria, Sudan and Libya? Why not at least a six month moratorium? If Americans have to wait in long lines at airport security, it is not unreasonable to make people from these countries wait longer for their visas so we can be reasonably sure they will not do us harm.

Related to this, America needs an increase in consular officers assigned to issuing visas and increased scrutiny and background checks for each applicant. There are U.S. embassies in some foreign countries where less than 5 minutes is average per applicant.

The second way that illegal immigrants enter the country is through the "back door" of slipping across our border. The United States has 93,000 miles coast line in addition to a 2000-mile border with Mexico and a 4000-mile border with Canada. There are 400 border agents on the Canadian border to cover 3 shifts and 4000 miles. We have Swisscheese borders without adequate policing.

We have been singing, "We are the World" more than we have been singing "America The Beautiful."

The gargantuan number of illegal aliens who come (mostly to find jobs, not engage in terror) undercuts national security and border control. The Clinton administration, with the tacit approval of much of corporate America, substantially crippled the interior enforcement of our laws against illegal immigration. We must better protect ourselves against illegal immigration so we can better protect ourselves against terrorists. Even though vast majority of the illegal aliens come seeking jobs, the enormous numbers of illegals prevent the U.S. from coming close to knowing who is legally in this country or not. It is essential to identify and remove the millions of aliens who enter legally and then stay on illegally as well as those who enter illegally from the start. If we can deny jobs to illegal aliens, we will not eliminate but we will go a long way towards reducing illegal immigration.

We need a national ID

For those who over-stay their visas we need a comprehensive ID reform that includes machine-readable visas and documents for all entrants to the U.S. to minimize forged entry documents, and a database of entry and exit information. An electronic work eligibility document will make it more difficult for unauthorized aliens to work and support themselves while in the U.S. Several pilot programs have been proven successful and must be made mandatory in all work places by Congress.

> *We are thousands of times more likely to be invaded by a foreign terrorist than a foreign country.*

What do we do about illegal immigrants who sneak across our border? I believe that border enforcement is not enough. I believe that we also need a national ID card. There is a simple and reliable system already in Germany, Austria, France, Greece, Spain, Hong Kong, Belgium and the Netherlands. Every citizen and lawful resident would be required to obtain a tamper-proof national identification card. It would be encoded with some type of biometric data—a fingerprint, retina scans, or voice pattern and have a hologram, like we see today on most drivers' licenses. Fingerprints or a retina scan is much harder to fake or forge than a picture. This ID will not only help us dramatically cut down illegal immigration, but will help with the growing problem of identity theft.

After a certain date, ID cards would help identify people here illegally two ways: First it will be impossible for people without ID cards to remain unseen through the American landscape. They would not be able to get on a plane, collect federal benefits, open a bank account, obtain health care, cash a check or get a job without a national ID. This is how most European countries help control their borders. For a foreigner, not having an ID card would be grounds for deportation. For all stops, detentions and arrests, police would require ID cards.

It is not adequate merely to have to show drivers' licenses or equivalent IDs issued by the state. Three of the nineteen Sept. 11th terrorists had Virginia IDs—issued under a permissive Virginia policy. I believe we must adopt a national standard for drivers license issuance and design. All states must protect these vital identity documents by cross-referencing them with the Social Security database and adopting anti-tampering laws.

We may choose to start with some sort of voluntary ID issued under uniform rules by states on a voluntary basis. This might be an alternative or a first step. A separate line at security gates could be available for those with a proper ID with a biometric identifier. If you wanted to avoid the long line, you would get a government issued ID.

   Understand that all U.S. citizens would also have to acquire and show the national identification card. For the average U.S. citizen, it would be little different than the present. When you get a job, cash a check, get on a plane, or collect a benefit, you will have to show your ID card instead of your driver's license. Police would still need reasonable suspicion to stop anyone. It would save American citizens billions in tax and welfare fraud and identity theft. It is not a silver bullet against terrorism; there is no silver bullet. It would not catch [Oklahoma City bomber] Timothy McVeigh or other citizen terrorists, but it would help us to start to get a handle on who is in our country legally.

   Then there is the question of legal immigration. In 1998, the United States took 7,883 immigrants from Iran; 2,220 from Iraq; 4,831 from Egypt; 13,094 from Pakistan, 2,840 from Syria, and 166 from Libya. The same question applies here as it does in the question of visas: Can we really do an adequate background check from places like Libya or Sudan?

   One of the most intriguing issues to me is the question of profiling. There is a lot of jerking of knees on the subject, but it seems to me that we should pay more attention to someone with a visa from a terrorist-supporting country than from Hong Kong or Peru. It would be public policy malpractice not to. It would not make sense in the name of non-profiling to check everyone equally. Some people are obviously more of a security risk than others. It may well be that an elderly Thai woman with a visa might cause us harm, but it is far less likely than someone with a visa from Libya, Iraq or the Sudan—or someone wearing an Osama bin Laden [the terrorist who masterminded the September 11 attacks] T-shirt.

   The famous military strategist Von Clausewitz observed that "Generals always fight the last war." Are we not doing the very same thing? We are thousands of times more likely to be invaded by a foreign terrorist than a foreign country. We need a military but we also need a border. The front line in this phase of warfare is the border. We ignore it at our peril.

13

Restricting Immigration Does Not Reduce Terrorism

Donald Kerwin

Donald Kerwin is the executive director of the Catholic Legal Immigration Network Inc. (CLINIC), a legal agency for 145 Catholic immigration programs.

Restricting immigration and otherwise harassing immigrants will hinder antiterrorism efforts. The people caught up in detention sweeps are overwhelmingly innocent and usually from nations that do not have ties to terrorism. Furthermore, actual terrorists will most likely not be caught in such sweeps, as they are usually chosen to be operatives precisely because they can blend into the general public. Turning away refugees and asylum seekers is a similarly ineffective antiterrorism method because it punishes people who are fleeing persecution and pose no terrorism threat. These policies instead hamper efforts to reduce terrorism, as they alienate immigrants who may be in the best position to help intelligence agencies gain access to communities they otherwise cannot infiltrate. Anti-immigration policies will have the most deleterious effect on immigrants who love America rather than on those who intend to harm it.

Over the [spring of 2003], thousands of Pakistani immigrants have abandoned their U.S. homes to seek refuge in Canada. Most wait fearfully in shelters and motels in U.S. border cities for their refugee interviews in Canada. The Immigration and Naturalization Service [I.N.S.] has arrested others who may or may not be released for their interviews. Most of the Pakistanis have lived in the United States for years, and many have U.S. citizen children. They have left behind good jobs and strong ties in their adopted communities. Since December [2002], 650 of them have come to a migrant shelter in Buffalo, N.Y. A typical family—a couple with two U.S. citizen children—arrived on a bleak day in mid-February [2003]. The couple had entered the United States on temporary visas in the early 1990's. They built a business that now employs 15 people. They have no ties in Canada, but they fear that their children could not survive deportation to Pakistan.

It should come as no surprise that Pakistanis and other immigrants no longer view the United States as a safe or fair country. [Since the September 11, 2001, terrorist attacks], targeted communities have seen thousands of their members arrested, detained for weeks without charge, held for immigration violations in a sweeping terrorism probe, called in for interviews and deported after closed hearings. Late [2002], the I.N.S. arrested and detained hundreds of immigrant men from five countries (most from Iran) who voluntarily came forward to register. The detainees had overstayed their temporary visas, although many awaited permanent residency based on approved family-based visas. Earlier [in 2003], the I.N.S. arrested men from another 13 mostly Middle Eastern countries. Pakistanis and Saudi Arabians comprise a third group of registrants. As their deadlines approached, the Pakistanis fled.

Al Qaeda recruits those who do not typically raise immigration "red flags"; its terrorists have overwhelmingly entered the United States in legal status.

The Bush administration has characterized its antiterror strategy as a measured attempt to protect liberty. Civil libertarians argue that it dishonors the U.S. constitutional tradition and amounts to a kind of surrender to terrorism. A greater risk, however, may be that immigrants increasingly view the war on terror as ineffective on its own terms and as a pretext to punish immigration violations. Their loss of confidence in the tactics and goals of the antiterror fight could prove fatal to its success.

The antiterror investigation

The government has justified its immigration enforcement measures based on contested theories of national security. According to experts in counterterrorism, the U.S. tactics result from intelligence deficiences and fear of unidentified Al Qaeda cells [that is, groups of terrorists] in the United States and Canada. Since Sept. 11, 2001, the government's priority has been to disrupt and prevent further attacks.

The Justice Department has likened its investigation to piecing together a "mosaic." Its guiding principle, says Vincent Cannistraro, former head of counterterrorism at the C.I.A., has been to "shake the trees and hope that something will fall out"—a strategy that in the short term "might have value and can disrupt terrorist acts, but whose success is difficult to prove." Intelligence experts have harshly criticized the Justice Department's tactics. As the former F.B.I. director William Webster told *The Washington Post*, pre-emptive arrest and detention "carries a lot of risk with it. You may interrupt something, but you may not bring it down. You may not be able to stop what is going down."

"Shaking the tree," moreover, can alienate targeted communities, push sources into hiding and deny investigators crucial information that they might acquire from monitoring suspects. If the "shaking the tree" approach netted a terrorist, it would be difficult to know this, much less to elicit information from him. "You can scare people," says Cannistraro, "which is actually what's being done, or you can try to win them over and cultivate good relationships with them. Cooperation and long-term relationships are much more successful."

Early in its antiterror investigation, the Justice Department adopted a zero-tolerance approach to immigration violations. In October 2001, Arab-American and Muslim-American leaders met with Attorney General John Ashcroft. The group had learned of immigrants who refused to report death threats and hate crimes because they feared deportation. The leaders asked that a "fire wall" be erected between federal hate crime investigations and immigration enforcement. Mr. Ashcroft rejected this request, however, saying that he would not excuse criminal conduct of any kind. For the participants, this represented a chilling development, signaling that violence against their out-of-status community members would go unreported and that cooperation in the broad antiterror fight could be punished.

Few idealize the presence (or treatment) of the seven million undocumented persons in the United States, but the undocumented do not present a heightened security risk. Nearly 80 percent come from Mexico and Latin America, not nations with a strong Al Qaeda presence. Furthermore, as Cannistraro points out, Al Qaeda recruits those who do not typically raise immigration "red flags"; its terrorists have overwhelmingly entered the United States in legal status. Thus, antiterror measures that target the undocumented—like sweeps of selected work sites and the use of state and local police to enforce immigration violations—do not effectively enhance security. On the contrary, they reduce the likelihood that the undocumented and their family members, who in many instances are U.S. citizens, will report crimes or assist in the terrorist investigation.

Secrecy

Secrecy has also characterized the antiterrorism investigation. For weeks, families, attorneys and consulates could not locate persons arrested in the post–Sept. 11 dragnet. Once located, many detainees could not be visited for extended periods. The Justice Department refused to release the names or even the exact number of those held. It categorically closed more than 600 deportation hearings deemed to be of "special interest." It warned federal agencies about disclosing information under the Freedom of Information Act. It authorized the monitoring of attorney-client communications that might be used to further terrorism.

The Justice Department maintains that secrecy is necessary to prevent terrorists from piecing together a mosaic of the investigation. It has even suggested that terrorists will not otherwise know when one of their members has been detained. Harry "Skip" Brandon, former head of counterterrorism for the F.B.I., argues that while certain investigative methods and sources need protection, the government often overstates its need for secrecy, sometimes keeping information from the public that could and should be disclosed. The government's failure to penetrate Al Qaeda and its resulting "woeful human intelligence," says Cannistraro, also casts doubt on the quality of the information that it seeks to keep secret. Secrecy can be counterproductive, since open hearings might prompt others to come forward with relevant information. It also insulates the government's tactics from public scrutiny and criticism.

The innocent

Only a few of the immigrants arrested in the antiterror probe have been charged with non-immigration crimes or deported on national security grounds. The F.B.I. has exonerated hundreds of others, but the Justice Department continues to label them potential security threats. During a conference in October 2002 that was co-hosted by [the Catholic Legal Immigration Network, Inc.], a Justice official reported that the government had deported some persons with suspected terrorist ties on the grounds of immigration violations, because their removal on national security grounds might have exposed investigative methods. The failure to prosecute suspected terrorists, he said, reflected the difficulty in securing convictions.

The Justice Department has offered a similar rationale for deporting Somali nationals. In response to class-action litigation challenging the Somalis' deportation to a land without a functional government, it claimed that not removing immigrants, "particularly to countries which are believed to harbor terrorists . . . runs the risk of jeopardizing national security." Furthermore, it argued that the removal of the Somalis on other than national security grounds did not mean that they lacked "knowledge of, or connection to, terrorism."

The refugee process may be the most improbable path that a terrorist could take to try to reach the United States.

While these claims cannot be verified or disproved, the release of suspected terrorists would contradict everything known about the Justice Department's investigation. "I feel strongly," says Brandon, "that if they had much of any information to go on, they would keep [suspected terrorists in their] custody and control. Once you deport them, you lose control over them." In addition, these statements cast suspicion on the overwhelming majority of detainees who have no terrorist ties. They might also lead to the punishment of innocent deportees in their countries of birth. Ironically, Justice officials refused to release the identities of the post–Sept. 11 detainees, in part because this might stigmatize them as potential terrorists.

Refugees and asylum seekers

The national security paradigm does not fit refugees, political asylum-seekers and others who are fleeing persecution. The refugee process may be the most improbable path that a terrorist could take to try to reach the United States. Yet after the Sept. 11 attacks, the United States halted refugee admissions for two months to review the program's security. By the year's end, only 27,000 of the 70,000 refugees approved for admission had entered the country. Advocates urged that unused refugee slots from 2002 be carried over to 2003, but [President George W. Bush] effectively lowered the admissions ceiling to 50,000 this year, reserving another 20,000 slots for use only in the event of regional shortfalls or overriding need. The pace of refugee admission has slowed in recent months—in the first quarter of fiscal year 2003, the United States allowed only 4,023 refugees to enter.

Any security concerns that threaten to eviscerate one of the United States' proudest programs—and one that directly assists the victims of terror—should be quickly resolved. "You need to vet refugees, like anybody else," says Brandon, "but processing small numbers is not a national security issue. It's an issue of government inefficiency or inadequate resources."

At worst, many of these restrictions undermine the anti-terror fight. At best, they do not go to the heart of the threat.

Similarly, Haitian boat people, fleeing persecution and poverty, do not present a terrorist threat. In late 2001, the administration began to detain Haitian boat people to deter others from coming. It subsequently announced that it would extend the harsh policies governing the Haitians to other immigrants. All non-Cuban undocumented migrants who have arrived by boat or have been in the country for less than two years will now be subject to expedited return. Even those who have established a "credible fear of persecution" will be detained. The Justice Department maintains that this policy will prevent mass migrations that could divert the Coast Guard from its national security duties. "This is not a national security measure per se," says Brandon, "and may be a misapplication of the national security rubric."

The Sept. 11 attacks also increased the momentum to harmonize U.S., Canadian and Mexican immigration enforcement policies. Mexican officials estimate that they annually intercept (with U.S. support) 250,000 migrants. It would imperil nobody to interview these migrants and to admit to the United States those who are fleeing danger. Nor does the recent U.S.-Canada safe-third country asylum agreement enhance security. Under it, a migrant who transits through one nation will not be able to seek asylum in the other. When implemented, this agreement will bar 15,000 Canadian asylum claims each year. With limited exceptions, these migrants will not be able to seek asylum in Canada and will be returned to the United States—an outcome that is at best security-neutral.

Reporting change of address

The war on terror has also given rise to law enforcement initiatives that, in a perfect world, might advance security but that the I.N.S. cannot accommodate. In July 2002 the Justice Department announced that it planned to enforce rigorously a law requiring immigrants to report changes of address within 10 days. This ignored the I.N.S.'s lamentable history of misplacing documents, including two million in a warehouse in Missouri, and its inability to assume new mandates. Most recently, a federal grand jury indicted two I.N.S. contractual employees in California for allegedly destroying tens of thousands of immigration applications. As the General Accounting Office recently reported, the I.N.S. "lacks adequate procedures and controls to ensure that the alien address information it receives is completely processed."

Since August [2003], the I.N.S. has received 825,000 change-of-address notices, compared to 2,800 in the previous month. It could not process the vast majority of these forms. Moreover, as the G.A.O. noted, immigrants who do not want to be detected will "not likely comply" with this requirement. Since the reporting program operates on an honor system, terrorists could simply provide false information.

Undermining anti-terrorism

Many immigrants understand terrorism intimately; they fled it. It outrages them that their adopted country has become a terrorist target. Immigrants will readily make sacrifices, endure hardships and support reasonable security measures. They have backed legislation to improve intelligence sharing, to track temporary visitors, to improve monitoring of foreign students and to tighten visa procedures. They have willingly cooperated with the F.B.I.'s investigation. Yet they increasingly reject the security rationale offered for immigration restrictions. At worst, many of these restrictions undermine the anti-terror fight. At best, they do not go to the heart of the threat. The United States needs to penetrate terrorist groups, improve human intelligence overseas and develop good sources and relationships with immigrant communities. Vincent Cannistraro puts it starkly: "If you have fingerprinted every Saudi in the United States and one then commits a suicide bombing, these [immigration] measures mean nothing."

14

Efforts to Make Air Travel Safe from Terrorists Have Failed

Nelson D. Schwartz and Julie Creswell

Nelson D. Schwartz and Julie Creswell are regular contributors to Fortune magazine.

Airports and airlines have failed to adequately protect their passengers from the threat of terrorism. Airports need to invest in smart fences that will surround airports and reduce the risk of shoulder-fired missile attacks. Security forces should also use biometric devices, such as palm, fingerprint, or retina scanners, to conduct reliable background checks on airline employees and passengers. Although it will cost billions of dollars to implement these and other innovations, safe air travel is worth it.

When the federal government promised after Sept. 11 [2001, when terrorists hijacked airplanes and flew them into the World Trade Center and the Pentagon] to make air travel safe and prevent terrorists from targeting more jetliners, frequent fliers probably had something in mind besides John Denehy. A Boston clam digger who works the muddy flats around Logan Airport, Denehy has been recruited by airport officials to keep his eyes peeled for suspicious characters. So if terrorists with shoulder-fired missiles decide to venture out in a rowboat and try to bring down a 747, they'd better watch out. "We're the best defensive wall against terrorists," says Denehy, hoisting a dripping bag of clams from his skiff. "We'd risk our lives to prevent anyone coming into contact with the runways who isn't supposed to be there."

Denehy's concern is admirable, and there's no doubt that he, like many Americans, is sincere about putting his life on the line to stop terror. But clam diggers aren't what's needed to protect America's skies. What is necessary—better cooperation among airlines, law enforcement, and federal agencies; new investments in everything from X-ray machines to smart fences around airports; and more sophisticated strategies to identify potential terrorists—is still years away. So a year and a half after the most devastating terrorist attack in history . . . flying is only modestly safer than it was on Sept. 10, 2001.

Safety and convenience don't have to be mutually exclusive.

Yes, stowed luggage is finally being inspected at U.S. airports, and the cockpit doors on commercial jets have been reinforced. But it's clear that the airlines and the newly created Transportation Security Administration (TSA) are still struggling to balance safety with convenience and for the most part delivering neither. Between the threat of another terrorist attack and the sudden spread of SARS,[1] the danger in the air has never seemed greater.

An industry in crisis

And the white-knuckle experience travelers face in the skies is matched by economic grimness on the ground. It will take billions to get things right, and both the federal government and the airlines are deep in debt already. Collectively, U.S. carriers have lost nearly $25 billion since 2001, more than they made in the previous five years. "It's been a quadruple blow—Sept. 11, the [2003] war in Iraq, the recession, and now SARS," says Representative John Mica, a Florida Republican who chairs the House Transportation Committee's panel on aviation. "It's a pretty serious situation."

Truth be told, flying really hasn't been fun or easy since the heyday of the jet set, when Pan Am was an American icon and people still donned coats and ties for a flight. But the current panic isn't just one of those periodic bouts of frustration Americans have experienced since air travel was deregulated in the late 1970s. The industry is in its deepest crisis ever—an estimated 100,000 jobs have been lost, two major carriers have gone bankrupt and a third could be headed in that direction, and the hub-and-spoke system that drove profits in the industry for the past two decades has turned into a money pit.

Some travelers have just given up flying for the time being—domestic air traffic [in April 2003] is down 15% from year-ago levels. To make matters worse, long-distance flights, one of the last sources of profits for carriers like United and Northwest, have been devastated by the SARS outbreak. Bookings between North America and Hong Kong have fallen 86% since early March, and United has cut flights between its Chicago hub and Tokyo by 50% in recent weeks.

Unfortunately, many business travelers don't have the luxury of staying on the ground, regardless of how inconvenient or dangerous flying has become. Teleconferencing and Internet confabs have taken the place of some business travel—adding to the airlines' problems—but often there's no substitute for a face-to-face meeting. Businessmen are still sucking it up

---

1. Severe Acute Respiratory Syndrome (SARS) sickened and killed people on several different continents during the winter of 2002. One of the ways it was spread was through travelers on airplanes.

and flying to Asia if that's what it takes to close the big deal. So when it comes to air travel, executives might as well be stuck in the middle seat.

But that doesn't mean things have to be as bad as they are now. The experience of security-conscious airlines like El Al, innovations at European airports like London's Heathrow and Amsterdam's Schiphol, and observations of security experts around the world show that safety and convenience don't have to be mutually exclusive.

We've talked to some of the smartest people in the industry about how to make life better—and safer—for business travelers. We can't promise you as much fun in the air as Leonardo DiCaprio had as a poseur Pan Am pilot in [the movie] *Catch Me If You Can*. But the ideas presented here could go a long way toward making air travel less of an ordeal than it's become.

Let's be straight—fixing the system won't be cheap or easy. It will require billions of dollars, along with considerable political capital, from Congress, the federal bureaucracy, the states, and the airline industry. Hard decisions will have to be made about privacy and civil liberties. The stakes for passengers, employees, and investors couldn't be higher. If air travel is made safe and sane again, a vital American industry can once more become an engine for economic and social mobility, as well as for shareholder profits. If it isn't, U.S. national security will be at risk, and business travelers might as well go Greyhound.

Before buying fancy technology, just build a fence

If there's one threat that has security experts alarmed these days, it's shoulder-launched missiles. When two of the rockets nearly brought down an Israeli airliner in Kenya [in 2002], it became clear that these cheap, plentiful, and easily transportable weapons are in the hands of terrorists, and that the near miss wasn't just a lucky break but a taste of things to come. "Even as we speak," says Mica, "those things are being smuggled across borders by people who have one interest—disrupting the air system and the U.S. economy."

> *Many airports consider bodies of water to be barriers to attack—as if terrorists couldn't use boats.*

But the most talked-about solution—installing expensive missile-deflection technology aboard every big plane—isn't necessarily the only answer. A much cheaper and quicker approach would be immediately to secure airport perimeters. "Most airports don't even have a simple fence," says Rafi Ron, who directed security at Israel's Ben Gurion airport before becoming a consultant to Logan and other U.S. airports. "It's something the TSA and airport authorities should take care of urgently." In fact, many airports consider bodies of water to be barriers to attack—as if terrorists couldn't use boats or even walk across shallow tidal marshes like the ones around New York City's airports.

What's needed are so-called smart fences, electronic barriers on land or under water that alert guards when breached. Ron estimates that it would cost about $10 million to $20 million for each smart fence, but even if they were installed at the top 200 airports, that's still less than the estimated $7 billion to $10 billion it would cost to equip the nation's jet-liners with antimissile defenses. And fences would address a host of other threats, such as hijackers and saboteurs. In the long run, missile defenses on planes may prove necessary too. But let's get those fences built now.

So what if he passed the background check?

It's one thing for the pretzel vendor and the airplane mechanic to get green lights on their personal histories, but who's watching them when they actually go to work? The TSA is beating its chest over the more than 800,000 background checks it has conducted on airport workers and con-cessionaires in the past year. The problem is, many of those workers don't go through the same security checkpoints and X-ray machines that pas-sengers do. "We have so many airports in this country where people who work on the aircraft and have access to critical areas never go through any security procedures," says Dawn Deeks, a spokesperson for the Associa-tion of Flight Attendants. "Denver is doing it right, but Chicago and Dal-las, for instance, are doing it wrong."

It's far easier to spot the bomber than pinpoint the bomb.

What's more, badges get lost and stolen all the time, and at most air-ports employees need only swipe a card or punch in a PIN number to ac-cess secure regions. The future is biometrics, a technology that requires a finger- or palm-print or a retina scan before an employee gains entry. "Everybody agrees that we need to move to biometrics, and some airports are already experimenting with those," says Charles Barclay, president of the American Association of Airport Executives. The holdup is that the TSA hasn't settled on a technology yet. While the TSA makes up its mind, bio-metric devices using palm geometry are already in operation at Tel Aviv's Ben Gurion airport, speeding returning travelers through passport control.

Get baggage screening out of the lobby

Logan's clam diggers-cum-terrorist spotters may not sound state-of-the-art. But the Boston airport has made dramatic improvements since Sept. 11, when it was the takeoff point for the two planes that struck the Twin Tow-ers [in New York City]. In addition to systematically searching for fake passports and training officers to spot suspicious behavior . . . , Massachu-setts authorities have developed one of the smartest baggage-screening sys-tems in the country. While passengers at most U.S. airports must put lug-gage through scanners as soon as they enter the terminal—creating the kind of lines normally associated with Rolling Stones concerts—Logan scans luggage after it's been turned over to the airline at the check-in desk. Bags are X-rayed on the same behind-the-scenes conveyors that move them to the plane. That saves time and lets passengers quickly head to the departure gate.

It wasn't cheap or easy—Massport, the state agency that runs Logan, spent $146 million and had more than 700 people working 24/7 last year to install 40 baggage scanners and 2.8 miles of new baggage belts. "We wanted to improve security, but we also felt that you had to take customer service into account," says Massport CEO Craig Coy. "The answer was incorporating baggage screening into the existing system, not creating another headache for passengers."

It has to be said: Searching little old ladies at security gates isn't a wise use of our thinly stretched resources.

You'd think that the powers that be would hand Coy a medal, but in fact he's still waiting for the TSA and the airlines to help pay for the new system—so far they've chipped in only $30 million of the $146 million tab. If Washington and the industry want people to start flying again, they should ante up for this kind of improvement at airports across the country.

Look for the bomber, not just the bomb

Remember all those National Guardsmen who appeared in airports after Sept. 11, standing around the X-ray machines with machine guns? Most are gone now, but the instinct to plunk down policemen in airports remains. Their presence looks reassuring but really doesn't do much to improve safety. A better idea would be to train security officers to move around, talking to passengers and looking for behaviors that might signal trouble.

That's exactly what's going on in Boston. Behavior recognition has long been used at Tel Aviv's Ben Gurion airport, and Rafi Ron introduced it in Boston [in the fall of 2002]. The principle is that it's far easier to spot the bomber than pinpoint the bomb. Massachusetts state troopers are trained to look for certain clues, like passengers who avoid eye contact or seem jittery. Police don't automatically arrest someone who's nervous; they just ask a few questions. If everything checks out, the passenger continues on his way. If something seems amiss, the trooper can ask to perform a more thorough search of the passenger and his luggage. It's not rocket science—what Ron calls a "targeted conversation" can take less time than taking off your shoes at the security checkpoint—but it's a much smarter way to deploy security personnel.

Profiling doesn't have to be a dirty word

It has to be said: Searching little old ladies at security gates isn't a wise use of our thinly stretched resources. Still, one of the most controversial efforts by the TSA is the development of a background-checking system called Computer-Assisted Passenger Pre-Screening II, or CAPPS II. Under the previous system, CAPPS I, each airline kept its own travel data and assigned a risk level to passengers based on criteria such as whether they purchased a one-way ticket or used cash.

CAPPS II, currently being tested by Delta with dummy data, will take passenger screening to a whole new level. Besides linking together all airline reservation systems, CAPPS II will also begin sifting through financial and government databases as soon as you buy a ticket. It will then assign you a risk level—green, yellow, or red. People given a yellow level will probably have to take off their shoes and have their carry-on bags swabbed for detection of explosives. "Red" means you'd better look into renting a car. "Terrorists are not normal people," says Ron, ticking off the kind of irregularities that might trip up a terrorist under CAPPS II—no long-term address, a series of new credit cards, or little credit history. The point about profiling is that it doesn't have to be ethnic—financial clues can be just as telling when it comes to detecting threats.

But of course CAPPS II is a hot button for civil-liberties activists who worry that the government would use it to discriminate against ethnic groups, and they want the program stopped immediately. They've even called for a boycott against Delta just for testing the system. Arnold Barnett, an MIT [Massachussetts Institute of Technology] professor who uses mathematical models to study aviation security, wonders how accurate such a database can be. "What if I subscribe to The Free Palestinian or if I have a college loan I never paid back? I may be a high credit risk but does that make me a terrorist threat?"

The critics raise good points, but there is a middle ground here. There are plenty of factors in a terrorist profile besides ethnicity or national origin. Indeed, the telltale financial signs CAPPS II looks for would have flagged the Sept. 11 hijackers. And even though it might have flaws, that's not a reason to kill CAPPS II before it's launched. In any case, Congress and the courts are going to have to decide—soon—how to balance civil liberties with the obvious terrorist threat to air travel. The bottom line is that some passengers pose more of a danger than others, as all those patted-down senior citizens can tell you. And CAPPS II is the best way for authorities to concentrate resources where they're needed most. . . .

You know us; let us through

Credit reports and bank statements? No problem. Last five addresses and the names of three previous employers? You got it. To avoid standing in line, some passengers are happy to provide that kind of information and are even willing to cover the cost of a deep background check. These people are what the airline industry calls Trusted Travelers, and creating a special card to identify them and let them zip through security is an idea that's been bandied about for years.

Plans to proceed with the Trusted Traveler came to a screeching halt after Sept. 11. Now, however, the TSA is requesting $5 million from Congress to research such a system. "Persons carrying such cards would be screened separately, using a less time-consuming level of security scrutiny," Carol Hallett, then-president of the Air Transport Association, told the California Chamber of Commerce last year. "The choice is up to the traveler—use a card or stand in line."

The Trusted Traveler program is a winner and should be put into practice as quickly as possible. We bet most business travelers (and probably many vacationers too) would happily turn over the information, avoiding the civil liberties headaches associated with CAPPS II. Privacy fanatics would be free to stand in line if they're concerned about handing over too much data to the authorities. Airlines and the TSA could speed customers onto planes, easing delays and boosting profits.

Of course, there are no guarantees that implementing Trusted Traveler or CAPPS II or anything else will make flying 100% safe and hassle-free. That's not how the world works in the post–Sept. 11 era. But adopting even a few of the measures outlined above would make air travel a bit more sane, not to mention secure. It will take money and hard work, but Washington and the airlines need to do something. Otherwise we'll have to rely on dumb luck—and on those Boston clammers.

15

America's Dependence on Foreign Oil Is Undermining Efforts to Reduce Terrorism

Gar Smith

Gar Smith is editor of the Edge, Environmental News *from the* Brink. *He writes regularly about political and environmental issues.*

The United States is the main target of global terrorism because its dependence on foreign oil forces it to maintain a resented presence around the world. Anti-American sentiment (a lead cause of terrorism) is fanned when America supports corrupt dictatorships in order to have access to oil. Additionally, because America buys oil from many countries that have ties to terrorism, Americans' own dollars end up lining the pockets of nations and individuals that support terrorism, which thoroughly undermines antiterrorism efforts. These ties must be cut. If it truly wants to reduce terrorism directed at it, the United States must wean itself off of foreign oil.

In the wake of the attacks on the World Trade Center and the Pentagon, [President] George W. Bush declared that America had been targeted "because we're the brightest beacon for freedom and opportunity in the world." Maybe there's another reason.

In his February 23, 1998 call for a "Jihad against the Crusaders," the wealthy Saudi-born militant Osama bin Laden argued that it was a religious duty "to kill the Americans and their allies—civilians and military" to force US soldiers "out of all the lands of Islam." He cited "three facts that are known to everyone."

• Bin Laden wrote bitterly of [Saudi Arabian] King Fahd's decision to invite thousands of US soldiers to establish a stronghold inside Saudi Arabia, the homeland of the holy Islamic City of Mecca. "For more than seven years," bin Laden wrote, "the US has been occupying the lands of Islam in the holiest of places . . . , plundering its riches, dictating to its rulers, humiliating its people, terrorizing its neighbors, and turning its bases . . . into a spearhead through which to fight the neighboring Muslim peoples."

• Bin Laden also railed against the US's "continuing aggression against the Iraqi people . . . despite the huge number of those killed, in excess of one million."

• Finally, he proclaimed that the real "aims behind these [US Middle East] wars are religious and economic," designed to "divert attention from [the] occupation of Jerusalem and murder of Muslims [in Palestine]."

In the aftermath of the September attacks, Reuters, the BBC and the Associated Press monitored public reaction throughout the Middle East in search of an answer to the question "Why was the US attacked?" The same three points came up repeatedly—Saudi Arabia, Iraq and Israel/Palestine. The consistency of these complaints should draw our attention.

US actions inspire attack

Writing in response to bin Laden's 1998 fatwa [religious edict] Ivan Eland, the Cato Institute's director of defense-policy studies, argued that the first goal of any nation's security policy should be "to protect citizens and property."

Eland noted that, "One of three terrorist attacks worldwide is directed against a US target. And that's not because the US is a rich capitalist nation. No, terrorists attack the US primarily for what it does, not what it is. . . . Because terrorist attacks are extremely difficult to prevent," Eland concluded, "the administration needs to concentrate its efforts on minimizing the motivation for such attacks in the first place. . . . Americans should not have to live in fear of terrorism just so Washington's foreign policy elite can attempt to achieve amorphous and ephemeral gains on the world chessboard."

Instead of taking the civilized course of tracking down the guilty parties and trying them before a world tribunal (as was the case in the Lockerbie airline bombing, the first World Trade Center bombing and the Beirut Marine barracks bombing), the Bush administration launched a massive aerial bombardment against Afghanistan [to oust the fundamentalist Afghan government known as the Taliban]. Such a response threatens to unleash the kind of endless escalation that Eland feared.

> *"Terrorists attack the US primarily for what it does, not what it is."*

The bombs, which initially were intended to destroy Afghan air defenses and assassinate the Taliban's leaders, soon wound up destroying Red Cross humanitarian warehouses, hospitals and homes. The sympathy that the world expressed for the US in September began to wane with the first photos of Afghan children whose bodies had been torn apart by cluster bombs. An investigation by University of New Hampshire Economics Professor Marc W Herold produced a shocking discovery: In the first 61 days of the US attacks, 3,767 Afghan civilians were reported killed by US bombs—a death toll that exceeded the revised estimates of the 3,000 civilians killed in the terrorist attack on the World Trade Center.

The military tactic of "massive retaliation" may not be an effective response to acts of terrorism. Israel provides a gruesome test-case. "If we have learned anything from Israel's treatment of the Palestinians," observes attorney Adam Gutride of A Jewish Voice for Peace, "it is that terrorism cannot be ended through retaliation, occupation or militarism."

A foreign policy based on oil

As John Bacher details in his article "Petrotyranny," there is one factor that links US foreign policy to Saudi Arabia, Kuwait and a rogue's gallery of repressive regimes, dictators, juntas and despots around the world. The glue that binds nearly every one of these unsavory alliances is the same: oil. Our foreign policy is captive to oil. The Pentagon runs on oil. Our position as a superpower is dependent on oil. The US has 200,000 troops stationed in 40 other countries, mostly deployed to secure our access to foreign oil. As Tom Cutler, the former head of NATO's [the North Atlantic Treaty Organization's] Petroleum Planning Committee, observed in the *Armed Forces Journal International*, the military's primary objective is not to maintain peace or safeguard liberty, but "to ensure adequate oil supplies for the national defense."

As author Barbara Kingsolver observed: "In the Persian Gulf War, we rushed to the aid of Kuwait, a monarchy in which women enjoyed approximately the same rights as a 19th-century American slave. The values we fought for and won there are best understood, I think, by oil companies."

As the Worldwatch Institute notes, the Pentagon is the world's largest oil consumer, burning "enough energy in 12 months to run the entire US urban mass transit system for almost 14 years." In peacetime, the US military consumes more than 150 million tons of oil annually.

Oil supplies approximately 34 percent of the world's energy needs but 79 percent of the Pentagon's energy. A US aircraft carrier burns 5,628 gallons per hour while a B-52 bomber swallows 3,612 gallons per hour. At full throttle, an M-1 Abrams tank burns through 252 gallons of fuel per hour while an F-15 on afterburners can torch 240 gallons per minute.

Like the weapons industry, the petroleum industry prospers on the revenue of conflict. Many members of the Bush administration were drawn from the ranks of the petroleum industry and the military-industrial elite. [Vice President] Dick Cheney's former employer, Halliburton, not only builds oil pipelines around the world, it also provides security for 150 far-flung embassies, supplies housekeeping services for US armed forces abroad and has recently begun offering teams of "privatized soldiers" to pump up the ranks of foreign armies.

Fight terrorism by reducing oil use

If the US economy were redirected to run on clean, renewable energy, we would not only be on the path to mitigating climate change, we would also be on the path to eliminating one of the major causes of terrorism. With towns, factories and homes powered by solar, wind and geothermal energy, no one country could dominate the world's energy-based economies.

Encouraging Americans to buy new automobiles to "keep America rolling" economically only encourages further oil dependence. Ultimately, the best way to counter the likes of Osama bin Laden is to reduce—or eliminate—the consumption of polluting petroleum fuels. As Yossef Bodansky, director of the Congressional Task Force on Terrorism and Unconventional Warfare, pointed out, bin Laden's funding comes from two main sources: Afghanistan's opium trade and $400 million in annual contributions from wealthy patrons in Saudi Arabia and other oil-producing states.

Energy conservation, fuel-efficient engines and renewable-energy technologies are already available. Unfortunately, no US government is likely to adopt this solution as long as oil money dominates the political landscape. Even with [former vice president] Al Gore in the White House, the US still might not have moved to relinquish its oil-based foreign policy since, to do so, would require the US to give up its position as the world's sole superpower. It is our control of oil supplies and the threat of our oil-powered military might that largely define the US as a superpower. . . .

A new foreign policy

Former New York Governor Mario Cuomo has joined the call for a "new foreign policy" that addresses the root causes of terrorism. Cuomo has challenged America to fight terrorism by responding to unmet human needs and to counter the "quiet tragedies" of injustice, poverty, hunger, inadequate healthcare and education that plague our world.

In an editorial essay penned one month before the September attacks, historian and author Chalmers Johnson noted with regret that the US, "as the lone surviving superpower, could have led through diplomacy and judiciously distributed foreign aid. . . . Instead, it has resorted most of the time to bluster, military force and financial manipulation. . . . American leaders believe that they are above the very concept of international law—unless defined and controlled by them. . . . History suggests that this country is riding for a big fall."

It is time to move to a world beyond oil, beyond repression and beyond superpowers. By demanding an economy based on clean, free renewable energy, we can replace our current outmoded foreign policy—based on military force, overseas bases, economic intimidation and political unilateralism—with a foreign policy based on human rights, social justice and environmental security.

While struggling to protect our freedoms at home, we must become actively involved in the debate over a new foreign policy. We need to campaign to stop the suffering of the innocent civilian population in Iraq. We need to call for the withdrawal of troops from Saudi Arabia and other countries where they are not welcome. We need to become more involved in finding solutions to the Israel-Palestine conflict.

Bush, Cheney and [U.S. attorney general John] Ashcroft have given Americans a choice: Are we prepared to sacrifice our freedoms for our foreign policy? Unfortunately, too many Americans appear all too willing to make that trade.

We must challenge the White House agenda, with its promise of endless war, more terrorist attacks and the steady erosion of our civil freedoms. A new world is possible, but we will now have to work harder to bring it about.

Organizations to Contact

The editors have compiled the following list of organizations concerned with the issues debated in this book. The descriptions are derived from materials provided by the organizations. All have publications or information available for interested readers. The list was compiled on the date of publication of the present volume; the information provided here may change. Be aware that many organizations take several weeks or longer to respond to inquiries, so allow as much time as possible.

American Civil Liberties Union (ACLU)
125 Broad St., 18th Floor, New York, NY 10004-2400
(212) 549-2500
e-mail: aclu@aclu.org • Web site: www.aclu.org

The American Civil Liberties Union is a national organization that works to defend Americans' civil rights guaranteed by the U.S. Constitution, arguing that measures to protect national security should not compromise fundamental civil liberties. It publishes and distributes policy statements, pamphlets, and press releases with titles such as "In Defense of Freedom in a Time of Crisis" and "National ID Cards: 5 Reasons Why They Should Be Rejected."

Anti-Defamation League (ADL)
823 United Nations Plaza, New York, NY 10017
(212) 885-7700 • fax: (212) 867-0779
Web site: www.adl.org

The Anti-Defamation League is a human relations organization dedicated to combating all forms of prejudice and bigotry. The league has placed a spotlight on terrorism and on the dangers posed by extremism. Its Web site records reactions to the September 11, 2001, terrorist incidents by both extremist and mainstream organizations, provides background information on terrorist Osama bin Laden, and furnishes other materials on terrorism and the Middle East. The ADL also maintains a bimonthly online newsletter, *Frontline*.

The Brookings Institution
1775 Massachusetts Ave. NW, Washington, DC 20036
(202) 797-6000 • fax: (202) 797-6004
e-mail: brookinfo@brookings.edu • Web site: www.brookings.org

The institution, founded in 1927, is a think tank that conducts research and education in foreign policy, economics, government, and the social sciences. In 2001 it began America's Response to Terrorism, a project that provides briefings and analysis to the public and which is featured on the center's Web site. Other publications include the quarterly *Brookings Review*, periodic *Policy Briefs*, and books including *Terrorism and U.S. Foreign Policy*.

CATO Institute
1000 Massachusetts Ave. NW, Washington, DC 20001-5403
(202) 842-0200 • fax: (202) 842-3490
e-mail: cato@cato.org • Web site: www.cato.org

The institute is a nonpartisan public policy research foundation dedicated to limiting the role of government and protecting individual liberties. It publishes the quarterly magazine *Regulation*, the bimonthly *Cato Policy Report*, and numerous policy papers and articles. Works on terrorism include "Does U.S. Intervention Overseas Breed Terrorism?" and "Military Tribunals No Answer."

Center for Defense Information
1779 Massachusetts Ave. NW, Suite 615, Washington, DC 20036
(202) 332-0600 • fax: (202) 462-4559
e-mail: info@cdi.org • Web site: www.cdi.org

The Center for Defense Information is a nonpartisan, nonprofit organization that researches all aspects of global security. It seeks to educate the public and policy makers about issues such as weapons systems, security policy, and defense budgeting. It publishes the monthly publication *Defense Monitor*, the issue brief "National Missile Defense: What Does It All Mean?" and the studies "Homeland Security: A Competitive Strategies Approach" and "Reforging the Sword."

Center for Immigration Studies
1522 K St. NW, Suite 820, Washington, DC 20005-1202
(202) 466-8185 • fax: (202) 466-8076
e-mail: center@cis.org • Web site: www.cis.org

The Center for Immigration Studies is the nation's only think tank dedicated to research and analysis of the economic, social, and demographic impacts of immigration on the United States. An independent, nonpartisan, nonprofit research organization founded in 1985, the center aims to expand public support for a an immigration policy that is both proimmigrant and low immigration. Among its publications are the backgrounders "The USA PATRIOT Act of 2001: A Summary of the Anti-Terrorism Law's Immigration-Related Provisions" and "America's Identity Crisis: Document Fraud Is Pervasive and Pernicious."

Center for Strategic and International Studies (CSIS)
1800 K St. NW, Suite 400, Washington, DC 20006
(202) 887-0200 • fax: (202) 775-3199
Web site: www.csis.org

The center works to provide world leaders with strategic insights and policy options on current and emerging global issues. It publishes books including *To Prevail: An American Strategy for the Campaign Against Terrorism*, the *Washington Quarterly*, a journal on political, economic, and security issues, and other publications including reports that can be downloaded from its Web site.

Central Intelligence Agency (CIA)
Office of Public Affairs, Washington, DC 20505
(703) 482-0623 • fax: (703) 482-1739
Web site: www.cia.gov

President Harry S. Truman created the CIA in 1947 with the signing of the National Security Act (NSA). The NSA charged the Director of Central Intelligence (DCI) with coordinating the nation's intelligence activities and correlating, evaluating, and disseminating intelligence that affects national security. The CIA is an independent agency, responsible to the president through the DCI, and accountable to the American people through the Intelligence Oversight Committee of the U.S. Congress. Publications, including *Factbook on Intelligence*, are available on its Web site.

Chemical and Biological Arms Control Institute (CBACI)
1747 Pennsylvania Ave. NW, 7th Floor, Washington, DC 20006
(202) 296-3550 • fax: (202) 296-3574
e-mail: cbaci@cbaci.org • Web site: www.cbaci.org

CBACI is a nonprofit corporation that promotes arms control and nonproliferation, with particular focus on the elimination of chemical and biological weapons. It fosters this goal by drawing on an extensive international network to provide an innovative program of research, analysis, technical support, and education. Among the institute's publications is the bimonthly report "Dispatch" and the reports "Bioterrorism in the United States: Threat, Preparedness, and Response" and "Contagion and Conflict: Health as a Global Security Challenge."

Council on American-Islamic Relations (CAIR)
453 New Jersey Ave. SE, Washington, DC 20003
(202) 488-8787 • fax: (202) 488-0833
e-mail: cair@cair-net.org • Web site: www.cair-net.org

CAIR is a nonprofit membership organization that presents an Islamic perspective on public policy issues and challenges the misrepresentation of Islam and Muslims. It publishes the quarterly newsletter *Faith in Action* and other various publications on Muslims in the United States. Its Web site includes statements condemning both the September 11 attacks and discrimination against Muslims.

Department of Homeland Security (DHS)
Washington, DC 20528
Web site: www.dhs.gov

The Department of Homeland Security was created in direct response to the terrorist attacks of September 11, 2001. Its creation was the the largest reshaping of the federal government since 1949. With this change, many formerly disparate offices became united in a mission to prevent terrorist attacks on American soil, reduce the country's vulnerability to terrorism, and effectively respond to attacks that did occur. The Department of Homeland Security took branches formerly of the Departments of Treasury, Justice, Agriculture, Energy, Commerce, Transportation, and Defense under its extensive wing. Services from the Coast Guard to Customs are now under the same umbrella, all with the singular mission of protecting the United States from attack. Among other information, the DHS Web site offers access to the Homeland Security Advisory System, a color-coded chart that indicates current terrorist threat levels.

Federal Aviation Administration (FAA)
800 Independence Ave. SW, Washington, DC 20591
(800) 322-7873 • fax: (202) 267-3484
Web site: www.faa.gov

The Federal Aviation Administration is the component of the U.S. Department of Transportation whose primary responsibility is the safety of civil aviation. The FAA's major functions include regulating civil aviation to promote safety and fulfill the requirements of national defense. Among its publications are *Technology Against Terrorism, Air Piracy, Airport Security, and International Terrorism: Winning the War Against Hijackers* and *Security Tips for Air Travelers.*

Federal Bureau of Investigation (FBI)
935 Pennsylvania Ave. NW, Room 7972, Washington, DC 20535
(202) 324-3000
Web site: www.fbi.gov

The FBI, the principle investigative arm of the U.S. Department of Justice, evolved from an unnamed force of special agents formed on July 26, 1909. It has the authority and responsibility to investigate specific crimes assigned to it. The FBI also is authorized to provide other law enforcement agencies with cooperative services, such as fingerprint identification, laboratory examinations, and police training. The mission of the FBI is to uphold the law through the investigation of violations of federal criminal law; to protect the United States from foreign intelligence and terrorist activities; to provide leadership and law enforcement assistance to federal, state, local, and international agencies; and to perform these responsibilities in a manner that is responsive to the needs of the public and is faithful to the Constitution of the United States. Press releases, congressional statements, and major speeches on issues concerning the FBI are available on the agency's Web site.

Institute for Policy Studies (IPS)
733 15th St. NW, Suite 1020, Washington, DC 20005
(202) 234-9382 • fax: (202) 387-7915
Web site: www.ips-dc.org

The Institute for Policy Studies is a progressive think tank that works to develop societies built around the values of justice and nonviolence. It publishes reports including "Global Perspectives: A Media Guide to Foreign Policy Experts." Numerous articles and interviews on September 11 and terrorism are available on its Web site.

International Policy Institute of Counter-Terrorism (ICT)
PO Box 167, Herzlia 46150, Israel
972-9-9527277 • fax: 972-9-9513073
e-mail: mail@ict.org.il • Web site: www.ict.org.il

ICT is a research institute dedicated to developing public policy solutions to international terrorism. The ICT Web site is a comprehensive resource on terrorism and counterterrorism, featuring an extensive database and terrorist attacks and organizations, including al Qaeda.

Islamic Supreme Council of America (ISCA)
1400 16th St. NW, Room B112, Washington, DC 20036
(202) 939-3400 • fax: (202) 939-3410
e-mail: staff@islamicsupremecouncil.org
Web site: www.islamicsupremecouncil.org

The ISCA is a nongovernmental religious organization that promotes Islam in America both by providing practical solutions to American Muslims in integrating Islamic teachings with American culture and by teaching non-Muslims that Islam is a religion of moderation, peace, and tolerance. It strongly condemns Islamic extremists and all forms of terrorism. Its Web site includes statements, commentaries, and reports on terrorism, including "Osama bin Laden: A Legend Gone Wrong" and "Jihad: A Misunderstood Concept from Islam."

National Security Agency
9800 Savage Rd., Ft. Meade, MD 20755-6248
(301) 688-6524
Web site: www.nsa.gov

The National Security Agency coordinates, directs, and performs activities, such as designing cipher systems, which protect American information systems and produce foreign intelligence information. It is the largest employer of mathematicians in the United States and also hires the nation's best codemakers and codebreakers. Speeches, briefings, and reports are available at the Web site.

U.S. Department of State, Counterterrorism Office
Office of Public Affairs, Room 2507, 2201 C St. NW, Washington, DC 20520
(202) 647-4000
e-mail: secretary@state.gov • Web site: www.state.gov

The office works to develop and implement American counterterrorism strategy and to improve cooperation with foreign governments. Articles and speeches by government officials are available at its Web site.

Bibliography

Books

Yonah Alexander — *Combating Terrorism: Strategies of Ten Countries.* Ann Arbor: University of Michigan Press, 2002.

Daniel Benjamin and Steven Simon — *The Age of Sacred Terror.* New York: Random House, 2002.

Kurt M. Campbell and Michele A. Flourney — *To Prevail: An American Strategy for the Campaign Against Terrorism.* Washington, DC: CSIS Press, 2001.

Wesley K. Clark — *Winning Modern Wars: Iraq, Terrorism, and the American Empire.* New York: PublicAffairs, 2003.

James X. Dempsey — *Terrorism and the Constitution: Sacrificing Civil Liberties in the Name of National Security.* Washington, DC: First Amendment Foundation, 2002.

Steven Emerson — *American Jihad: The Terrorists Living Among Us.* New York: Free Press, 2002.

Kathlyn Gay — *Silent Death: The Threat of Chemical and Biological Terrorism.* Brookfield, CT: Twenty-first Century Books, 2001.

Samuel M. Katz — *Relentless Pursuit: The DSS and the Manhunt for the Al-Qaeda Terrorists.* New York: Tom Doherty, 2002.

Richard Mintzer — *Keeping the Peace: The U.S. Military Responds to Terror.* New York: Chelsea House, 2002.

National Research Council — *Making the Nation Safer: The Role of Science and Technology for Countering Terrorism.* Washington, DC: National Academies Press, 2002.

Todd S. Purdam and the *New York Times* — *A Time of Our Choosing: America's War in Iraq.* New York: Times Books, 2003.

Roger Scruton — *The West and the Rest.* Wilmington, DE: Intercollegiate Studies Institute, 2002.

Jeffrey D. Simon — *The Terrorist Trap: America's Experience with Terrorism.* Bloomington: Indiana University Press, 2001.

Strobe Talbott and Nayan Chanda, eds. — *The Age of Terror: America and the World After September 11.* New York: Basic Books, 2001.

Gore Vidal — *Perpetual War for Perpetual Peace: How We Got to Be So Hated.* New York: Thunder's Mouth Press, 2002.

Howard Zinn — *Terrorism and War.* New York: Seven Stories, 2002.

Periodicals

William M. Arkin — "'War' Plays into Terrorists' Hands," *Los Angeles Times*, December 29, 2002.

Bruce Buena de Mesquita — "Questions—and Answers," *Hoover Digest*, Winter 2002.

Daniel Byman — "Scoring the War on Terrorism," *National Interest*, Summer 2003.

David Cole — "National Security State," *Nation*, December 17, 2001.

Kevin Coonan — "One Year Later," *Trauma Reports*, November/December 2002.

Ruth David — "Homeland Security: Building a National Strategy," *Bridge*, Spring 2002.

Larry Diamond — "How to Win the War," *Hoover Digest*, Winter 2002.

Economist — "Two Years On; the War on Terror," September 13, 2003.

William A. Galston — "The Perils of Preemptive War," *Philosophy & Public Policy Quarterly*, Fall 2002.

Scott Gottlieb — "Wake Up and Smell the Bio Threat," *American Enterprise*, January/February 2003.

Denis Hayes and Lisa A. Hayes — "Oil and Power," *OnEarth*, Winter 2002.

Scott Holleran — "Why We're Losing the War on Terrorism," *Capitalism Magazine*, September 8, 2003.

Derrick Z. Jackson — "U.S. Plays the Arms Sales Game," *Liberal Opinion*, March 2, 2003.

Khalid Khawaja — "War Will Create More Baby Osama bin Ladens," *Los Angeles Times*, March 2, 2003.

Michael T. Klare — "Oil Moves the War Machine," *Progressive*, June 2002.

Charles Krauthammer — "The Case for Profiling," *Time*, March 18, 2002.

Nelson Lund — "The Conservative Case Against Racial Profiling in the War on Terrorism," *Albany Law Review*, Winter 2002.

Heather Mac Donald — "Total Misrepresentation," *Weekly Standard*, January 27, 2003.

John O'Sullivan — "May We Get Serious Now?" *National Review*, April 22, 2002.

Ramesh Ponnuru — "1984 in 2003?" *National Review*, June 2, 2003.

Bill Powell — "Are We Safe Yet?" *Fortune*, September 16, 2002.

Jeffrey Rosen — "Tapped Out," *New Republic*, October 15, 2001.

Jonathan Schell — "The Importance of Losing," *Nation*, September 22, 2003.

Gary Schmitt — "Can the CIA and the FBI Meet the Threat?" *World & I*, October 2002.

Peter Schwartz and   "How Hydrogen Can Save America," *Wired*, September
Doug Randall   26, 2003.

Jessica Stern   "How America Created a Terrorist Haven," *New York
                      Times*, August 20, 2003.

Bruce J. Terris   "Common Sense in Profiling," *Midstream*, February/
                      March 2002.

Douglas Waller   "The CIA's Secret Army," *Time*, February 3, 2003.

Howard Zinn   "Operation Enduring War," *Progressive*, March 2002.

Index